Early Raves about
Humorous Letters From the Edge

"Erma Bombeck has a male soul mate. If laughter is the best medicine, Bill has cured me of all my ills. Each page tickled me to the point that I can't stop chuckling on elevators, in traffic, and at board meetings. America needs this kind of relief. I'm giving one to everyone I know."

—**Dr. Denis Waitley, author,** *Seeds of Greatness*

"A witty and heartfelt tale of a family of East Coast transplants who find paradise with an (almost) ocean view. Bill Seaton makes every day seem like Christmas."

—**Larry Himmel, San Diego CBS affiliate KFMB-TV**

"Verrry interesssting...and also a barrel of laughs if you have an empty one around."

—**Arte Johnson (Wolfgang Busch),** *Laugh-In*

HUMOROUS LETTERS
FROM THE EDGE

Chronicles of a Crazy Clan

Bill Seaton

To Barbara —

Happy Holidays! May you live long — and die laughing!

GREEN FLASH
PUBLISHING
SAN DIEGO, CALIFORNIA

Best wishes,

Bill Seaton

First printing 2003

ISBN 0-9726013-2-5
LCCN 2002114694

ATTENTION CORPORATIONS, PROFESSIONAL ORGANIZATIONS: Quantity discounts are available on bulk purchases of this book for gift purposes. Special books or book excerpts can also be created to fit specific needs. For information, please contact Green Flash Publishing, 3466 Larga Circle, San Diego, CA 92110; ph. 619-222-9982.

Dedication

to
Lovae

a beautiful homemaker, cook, electrician,
plumber, gardener, and carpenter,
mother of my four all-American children
(but always claimed she raised *five* kids),
and
who could never understand why people
found these letters humorous every year.

Table of Contents

Introduction

Every week, thousands of modern-day pioneers flock to Southern California with starry-eyed hopes and a U-Haul trailer, bent on taking up residence in the Promised Land.

However, my announcement in the summer of 1959 that I planned to pack up the family and do the same was greeted with about the same enthusiasm one usually sees displayed for a third-stage smog alert.

It shocked everyone. Especially my wife Lovae. I believe the little woman's exact words were, "Are you nuts?" as she went off to bed.

Relatives referred to it as temporary insanity.

My mother couldn't believe anyone bearing her genes would be crazy enough to leave a good PR job in Washington, DC, and uproot their well-ensconced suburban family to move 3,000 miles, like "Oakies," with no promise of employment. She said it might have been better if she'd never brought my basket in off the door stoop.

My brother, Mark, was equally supportive. "Why the devil would you want to go to California?" he asked. "Everyone out there is either on drugs, in therapy, or practicing to be a serial killer."

I told my boss, in resigning, that as a young writer and movie buff, I hoped to get a shot at Hollywood sometime before social security kicked in. "Hollywood dashes more dreams than an alarm clock," he scoffed.

Lovae's mother, Dawn Oakley, a nearby neighbor in suburban Virginia, wondered if maybe I didn't belong over at St. Elizabeth's with the loony poet, Ezra Pound, when she heard our exciting news.

I guess you could say she had me figured as a cerebral tortoise from the get-go. That would have been after my first date with her startlingly-beautiful 17-year-old daughter. When we'd shown up at 2:00 A.M., *well* past school-night curfew, Dawn had rather vehemently threatened to shoot me!

Lacerated in my memory, understandably, is a vision of mother Oakley waiting on the porch under a chilly moon. She was wearing a faded Chenille robe, hair in pin-curls, face a shade of red I had never encountered before, announcing, loud enough to startle birds out of trees, that not only was she not interested in meeting me, but should she ever see my silly 18-year-old Great Plains face at her door again, she would send me back to my Potomac River naval barracks with a 22-slug in a delicate part of my anatomy. I wasted no time catching the last public transportation back to DC.

So, after I left the Navy and married her daughter 10 months later, it took a few years of stroking, and proof I could hold a job more than six months, to finally win her over.

Now *this*.

Dawn couldn't imagine how we would survive, having invited us almost weekly to big dinners, sending home the left-overs, and enabling us to keep the kids well fed when I *had* a job.

Looking back some 50 years later, I suppose it did seem like a mindless thing to do.

Maybe even stupid.

But Lovae and I had often dreamed—as beach lovers and barbecue addicts—of year-round outdoor life under swaying palms. Especially during the early years of our teen-age marriage. The dream had diminished with the first and second pregnancies. And had been completely obliterated after a third child magically appeared.

So it was a humid July evening in Washington, DC, when I followed up on my shocking Westward-Ho pronouncement.

"Honey, the world belongs to the brave," I chirped tritely, while Lovae sat rigidly staring out the window. "Think of the pioneers—they didn't know what lay ahead! We're just like them. Without the Indians."

I began to stroke her hair. "We're 30. When did we last have a *real* adventure?"

She guessed either the Washington's Birthday 1-cent sale, or the evening our three- year-old surreptitiously placed a can of unopened peas in the oven and redecorated the kitchen.

The next morning, heavily caffeined, the little woman gazed into her Corn Flakes and sighed, "All right, Columbus, get the covered wagon and let's have a great adventure. I guess we can only starve once."

And neither of us would miss Washington's humid summers and shut-in winters with viruses A through Z, we agreed, hugging and dabbing at each other's tears.

The children—Sherrie, nine, Deborah, eight, and Craig, three—soon began to share our excitement. ("Daddy, can we go to Disneyland every week? Will we have horses?")

"Yes, children, if Daddy wins lots of money in Las Vegas!" Lovae would chime in with a little more sarcasm than I thought necessary.

On the eve of our departure, Lovae sat down with pencil and paper and produced a schematic drawing, showing how each piece of furniture we owned would fit into a 10-foot U-haul trailer.

Relieving me of the evening paper, she announced that two fast-stepping young bucks (friend John Ford had been recruited) could complete the task in under three hours.

As it turned out, three slightly spent braves, moving just short of a trot, completed the loading in seven hours. We all stared hollowly around 1:00 A.M. at the couch, two straight-back chairs, a child's chest of drawers, gooseneck lamp, and wringer-washer, which would not mathematically fit into the already crammed load.

The problem solved by an 8:00 A.M. sidewalk auction, attended by a half-dozen scrapping neighbors, we said our goodbyes and drove to Dawn's big house in nearby Arlington for a final breakfast. All agreed there would be no tears; our last moments together were to be happy ones. We downed a hearty breakfast on the terrace, smoked, recalled good times—then everyone had a hysterical cry.

We blew noses, crawled into the car, and after a snappy 10 minutes of rearranging gear and heated discussions over whose legs were to go where, the '55 Chevy groaned away into the Golden West. Lovae waved bravely, certain she would never see her folks again.

It was a fun trip. Similar to the one Napoleon made to Russia. Pulling 2,000 pounds, the rear bumper exactly 3 inches off the pavement, and with cameras, magazines, maps, a huge cooler, a bale of Kleenex, 4 pillows, 2 throw rugs, a stray suitcase, 11 dolls, 3 half-decks of cards, guns, balloons, 14 pencils, bananas, crackers, several dozen loose crayons and books, and all three children settling down to some serious scrapping, we blissfully set off down the wrong highway.

It was, of course, *her* fault. We didn't speak again while searching for the correct carefully preplanned route.

Our mileage the first day wasn't much over that of a covered-wagon train. The trusty Chevy Six, which the girls dubbed "The

Rocket," sagged and groaned pathetically under the 2,000-pound load. We averaged a disconcerting 28 mph through the foothills of Pennsylvania.

In four hours we made all of 100 miles.

I stopped every 20 miles or so to check the load…and the boiling tires. The merry adventurer had grown super-cautious. My biggest fear was of a blowout or a transmission problem. No mechanic, I admittedly didn't know a transmission from a nine-banded armadillo.

All sensed my apprehension. When we hit a stretch of dangerously winding road in the foothills, everyone fell silent. The scene was grim.

"Well, only 2,900 miles to go," I sang out when we had finally negotiated the grade. But I felt terrible when the three-year-old wanted to know exactly what we had done with his bed and how many hours to California? Also, what *was* California?

The gas tank sank from full to empty in the shortest time this side of the Indianapolis Speedway. We estimated with some alarm, that we were reeling off a whole 9 miles per gallon. One trailer wheel began to wobble. The engine developed a new knock. I weighed the pros and cons of stopping and sending Lovae and the children by bus back to her Mother's.

But our worries lifted as we reached the wonderfully straight turnpike. I soon eased the needle up to 55 mph and sat back, sighing deeply, the epitome of relaxation.

Then Debbie exploded a balloon in the backseat. I was a quarter-of-a-mile getting us back onto the road again! A firm edict ensued to the effect that there would "by-damn" be no more balloon-blowing this trip!

By late afternoon, the asphalt was a shimmering inferno. We decided to take refuge in a half-finished, but air-conditioned, motel with an attractive pool. In a weak moment, we agreed the adults would stand the kids in a game of water basketball. The adults were 20 points behind when a Midwestern–type blow came up and blew chairs and umbrellas all over town.

We fled, dripping, to the room, where animal-like noises could soon be heard as our famished band devoured a dinner of cold chicken, beans, and potato salad—quickly produced from the life-restoring cooler (where Dawn had hidden $20 under the beans). No Chateaubriand ever tasted better. In the middle of *Gunsmoke*, five bodies relaxed completely out of the picture.

After sleeping in late when the Reliable Motel forgot our 7:00 A.M. wake-up call, we packed, invigorated and carefree. As we cruised along in the warm, fragrant August morning, I felt younger and more vital than I had in ages. We were all soon jabbering of warm winters, Hollywood, and white, sandy beaches.

Then we turned around and returned for the big water jug left behind.

In Ohio, we stopped often for roadside snacks, to gas up, go potty (once after a watermelon, we averaged a filling station every 25 miles), for map consultation, and to check the trailer. We even stopped to read historical markers and were eyed suspiciously by passing Highway Patrol.

That afternoon a black sky, which would have turned Balboa back, teamed up with tornado-like winds to ravage the area. We dropped anchor and waited in the mud for the end. The children clung to our necks as the car and trailer rocked with each fierce gust. Fortunately the twister hit elsewhere. We made fast tracks out of there.

Singing "You Are My Sunshine" slightly off-key, we reached Indianapolis at dusk and a storm of such intensity the streets flooded over the sidewalks. Again, we pulled off and waited, now gravely doubting the wisdom of leaving our cozy habitat in Virginia.

That evening, as an ominous darkness fell, we stopped early at a small motel; because the wind whipped the trailer so violently, I had trouble keeping the car on the road.

We unloaded in a cold drizzle. Hauling the 58 items from the car and trailer each night was not what an orthopedic doctor would recommend for already ailing backs.

I squish-squashed in with my last load just as the smiling, white-haired proprietor was setting up a cot. Little Craig chose that moment to blurt out: "Hey, Dad, when can we have beer?" In an ill-advised decision the night before, we had permitted several sips from my glass to induce sleep. The manager, who looked like the local deacon, straightened, rolled his eyes, and solemnly marched out (to report to Social Services, I supposed).

The next morning, after we breakfasted and loaded the gypsy caravan, Lovae developed hay fever and came close to expiring right there amidst the fields of oats and corn. In between wracking sneezes, she broke up arguments and explained to Craig where the sun and moon go, where his bed was, and where *we* were actually going. "Why don't we just go home?" he would conclude. She smiled and blew her nose, then took the wheel and drove the next few hundred miles while I cowered in back.

Necessity is—a mother. Plowing through Oklahoma, she ran the right wheels off the trail. This evoked a certain amount of screaming from all passengers but no noticeable damage. So much for my nap.

Debbie, the youngest girl, was the first of our intrepid band to drop. She had hurled her breakfast in Kansas and complained of severe pain. We frantically searched out a hospital at the next small town and delivered her to the emergency room. After anxious moments over the possibility of appendicitis, food poisoning, etc., a doctor appeared, reporting that she was "as healthy as he was," while jovially writing out a hefty bill.

Then after an overnight stop in Oklahoma to visit Lovae's sister and storm cellar, we ventured on and soon found ourselves in the *real* West. For some reason, our reaction was to eat ravenously, just like we were employed. Craig was switched quickly to the Coke-and-cracker diet upon showing signs of paleness. I sunburned my elbow. Lovae began to look a bit wild-eyed from the children's playful arguing and her chin-on-knees position while "riding shotgun."

We made stops at the Painted Desert and the Meteor Crater in Arizona. Craig upchucked 1,500 feet down the great crater. That completed the educational portion of our journey.

It didn't, however, complete *my* contribution. After a careful study of the map, I cleverly drove us down a road that must have been an abandoned Apache trail. By the time we realized it, darkness had fallen and we were nearly out of gas. All grew alarmed. Craig hunkered down and cried out, "An Indian will kill me!" But I heroically found a turn that led us back to civilization.

Fleeing colorful Arizona, we zoomed 40 miles downhill (actually) to Needles, California, the famous jump-off point to the desert. We stopped to gas and replenish the water jugs. Seeing cars with trailers like ours, others with beds and bicycles strapped to the top, kids hanging out of the windows, license plates from all states, everyone gassing up, filling water coolers, checking tires to start the night trek across the boiling desert—I was suddenly filled with a sense of adventure, the way I had promised it would be.

It is difficult to describe, but in spite of our looking like characters out of *The Grapes of Wrath*, we felt a child-like excitement at being a part of this crazy American pursuit of the eternal sun in the Promised Land.

At 9:00 P.M., when the desert cooled, we wished fellow travelers luck and nudged The Rocket out into the 98-degree heat. The engine temperature needle soared within minutes to just this side of boiling. We watched, pop-eyed.

But it eased off later as we roared downhill to the desert floor. The air was hot and dry. Our lips began to crack, and we sipped Cokes and took off our shirts and put ice-cubes on our necks. Flares at the sides of the road warned against going off onto the soft shoulders. I kept thinking it would break our spirit if we had tire trouble at that moment. But the desert sky was crystal clear with a million stars.

We kept looking up and silently, I guess, asked for help and guidance just a little longer. And with the aid of a thermos of coffee and gallons of water for the Chevy, we roared out of the Mojave oven intact.

By the time we had cruised down the Los Angeles Freeway and plowed into Inglewood with only one wrong turn, we felt deep in our beings that California was where we belonged. There were no photographers, or flags to plant, but we spilled from the car, qualified as pioneers, 1959 stock…us and 1,999 other families that day.

When down to our last pound of hamburger, I landed a job that has led to a fascinating 40-some-year career in San Diego.

I began writing annual year-end holiday chronicles of life in California to friends and family in the East. These humorous personal essays, to some degree, capture the essence of the times in the '60s, '70s, and '80s in Southern California as we enjoyed our palm trees, sandy beaches, and year-round barbecues.

I have compiled a collection of them here in hopes others will enjoy and get a chuckle or two.

Holiday Cheers!

1960

Well, look at us—survived our first full year in California! Drop your packages, grab some caffeine, and I'll hit a few highlights.

I can still visualize a morning last spring, the vehicle I was trapped in careening over winding mountain roads on the way to Palm Springs. My new employer was driving, an open can of Bud precariously balanced in the middle of the steering wheel, his eager eyes searching the distant rocky landscape. I sat tensely in the "death seat," poised to grab the wheel, if necessary, to prevent our plunge into the bleak desert canyons several thousand feet below.

"Ever seen a Bighorn sheep in the wild?" Charlie "Ram" Ramsey, ad agency chief and a famed outdoorsman, asked— miraculously keeping the speeding car from becoming airborne while he drained another swallow.

"No," I confessed, a city boy who had seldom seen anything wilder than squirrels in the park, or a mouse in the cupboard in my recent city of employment, Washington, DC.

"I've tracked them in Baja," he said, with a far-away look. "They're something, kid, I'll tell you." I nodded, trying to look

11

interested. My mind was actually on a PR campaign for the new client we were about to meet, regarding plans to build a desert retirement city.

Ram squinted out his window again. "I've heard there are a few in these mountains—but I've never spotted one."

"I'll be glad to keep an eye out," I replied wildly, concerned about leaving three needy youngsters fatherless. "Here, let me hold that brew for you, sir—while we descend from 4,000 feet."

I started working for this colorful character in January as assistant PR director of the town's largest advertising agency, just six months after my cross-country trek to relocate from the East.

He's quite a contrast to the military, press, and congressional types I worked with the past seven years in the nation's capital. A salesman nonpareil, inevitably clad in a Brooks Brothers suit, pants featuring a 32-inch waist, and gleaming motorcycle rider's buckle, he often has a sizeable chaw in his lip, holds the world-record for hauling in a sailfish on a 6-pound test line, and can often be seen paddling his kayak around in the early morning mist of the Pacific.

I've signed on with a talented, but somewhat eccentric, nonconformist:

> The only exec I know who dips snuff…
> or has beer *on tap* at home…
> or catches fish bigger than my eldest…
> or lifts weights before breakfast…
> or tracks bighorn sheep in Mexico.

I sit so often in admiration as this tanned, disarming agency exec mesmerizes clients with his folksy oratory and story-telling, periodically pausing to punctuate a point with a spat out the conference room door into his landscaped atrium, nailing a wee tree bent as if trying to avoid another of his deliveries.

I was hired, basically, to keep a dry diaper on a demanding, but important, client. Rumor has it that Ram, in need of a sacrificial lamb, directed personnel to "seek out that young writer who applied here a few months ago—those guys from the East have a good work ethic." (That's me, folks!)

They tracked me down at the dead-end job I had reluctantly taken, after landing, jobless, in San Diego during poor economic conditions. I reported for an interview in awe of the agency's ivy-covered, one-story redwood building tucked away on a corner residential lot.

I'd have worked for nothing after seeing the dazzling blonde receptionist.

In his office, the no-nonsense VP of Public Relations stared through thick glasses at my resume, while I sat like Lincoln. He looked up sharply and asked one key question, "How many news releases would you say you wrote a year for the National Association of Realtors?"

When I exaggerated and said it must have been about a hundred, he said, "You're hired!" No checking references, former employers, or the FBI. A 10-minute interview and *boom*! I was in the agency business. Welcome—and bring a case of Pepto-Bismol.

This fall, Lovae and I celebrated our fourth year without a pregnancy by buying a new home in Point Loma, featuring green wall-to-wall debt. But the cactus juice they drink around here makes just about everything look do-able.

Four bedrooms and 1,700 square feet with open beam ceilings, our casa's about 10 minutes from the beach, as the crow flies. If you're walking—it's more like an hour and a half. Lovae seems ecstatically happy to have permanent shelter and polishes it as if it were a diamond. You know how women are about having a fine nest. Makes them less likely to throw things when you show up late for dinner.

Our summer vacation was necessarily short and sweet. We took the kiddies, Sherrie, now a tall 10, Debbie, 9, and Craig, 4, to the nearby mountains, setting up camp at Lake Arrowhead's

Village Inn, appealingly situated in Swiss-like surroundings. We sniffed the pine needles and swam and fished and boated. Then the kids kept everyone in the hotel up all night.

On the way back, we visited Santa's Village at nearby Big Bear and Craig asked Santa for a cowboy, and we swung down to Hollywood to see an old Navy shipmate, John Moen, and spent the afternoon at the home of one of his producer friends (who apparently hadn't produced much since Gene Autrey last rode into the sunset).

Returning by way of Hermosa Beach, we spent a few days with the Sorensens, high school pals, and swam in the red tide, and watched the phosphorus waves at night. We sipped our tequila and wondered how we ever survived winters in Iowa. The rest of the year, too.

We are hooked on water. We spend every free weekend riding cool breakers at the beach with the kids and the rest of the week catering to their awesome appetites. They are becoming expert swimmers (in a pool we use), and Craig draws a crowd diving off the board—often on my head.

Also, I've started playing tennis twice a week with guys from the office. Hope to soon get it over the net twice consecutively.

I took Lovae to Tijuana for her first bullfight (I'd seen a few the spring I lived in Majorca). She was quietly horrified at all the blood. And we both agreed that the wild ride back to the border in a taxi with broken springs, over potholes, and on the wrong side of the road, was infinitely more thrilling. The wine stains from trying to drink out of one of those leather things won't come out of my bullfight shirt.

I mentioned the retirement community a client is building in Palm Springs. I took wifey over there on business the week Liz Taylor was supposed to be sitting around the desert sweating out the evil. We didn't see Liz, but held a ground-breaking ceremony in a driving sandstorm, then drove back next day through the mountains in a snowstorm, the first we'd seen in two years.

We returned eagerly to our Harbor in the Sun (and a short, snappy cold wave).

But Sunday we were swimming again, and the Sorensens drove down to help trim our big tree. It took much work, and Roy and I enjoyed watching while we killed the Christmas cheer.

The year ended by the family appearing in some holiday newspaper publicity shots for a client, and Sherrie portraying the lovely "Mary" in the school Nativity program. She looked so angelic, I sniffled into my hanky, seeing our "baby" playing grown-up like that. I went home and plucked a gray hair from my chest.

We all wish we could hop a plane and visit with you for the holidays—it's been a long, long time, as the song goes. Maybe you'll come see us in the coming fabulous months.

I leave you with this thought for the New Year: "In the great game of you against the world, always bet on the world."

Yuletide Greetings...

Our fourth Christmas in seaside San Diego, just a pinata's toss from the Mexican border. My sunburn smarts a little.

I still can't get used to Christmas shopping in shorts after years of freezing my kneecaps off while following the snow plow to stores in the East for my usual last-minute gift.

The year did start with a bit of unusual weather—a freak hail storm. Our neighbor's six-year-old son had never seen hail or snow. As he stood in the front window, listening to hail pelt the roof, watching the lawn magically turn white, he called out forlornly, "Mom, are we all going to die?"

This week, we've been hiding out from neighborhood holiday parties (which we probably wouldn't have been invited to anyway). We've had enough. We partied two nights in San Francisco, and then were invited for some reason to a champagne gala in a La Jolla estate that had an eye-popping view of the Pacific. All the shiny cars parked out front made it look like a Caddy-Mercedes sales lot. Lovae and I found a place for our '55 Chevy down the street.

On the way home, we stopped at a little neighborhood store for milk and cigarettes. A sign in the front window said: "Open

24 Hours." As I got out, a guy with a gray ponytail was just locking the door. "Why are you closing up?" I asked. "Your sign there says open 24 hours."

"But not consecutively," he replied.

It's been an amazing year, looking back:

> Amazing that in January we'll be having our fourth child by the fourth different birth-control method;

> Amazing how a boy kid can wear out the *tops* of his shoes every five weeks;

> Amazing how Chapter One is the sum total of the novel I started to write last year;

> Amazing how when I sit down to write, the TV goes on in my ear, the phone rings, and I get thirsty;

> Amazing that we actually lured a pro grid team down here from LA (and I got a client to pledge the largest ticket buy!);

> Amazing how long two kids can argue (not as long as three);

> Amazing how often I had to travel to Palm Springs and San Fran in my PR job;

> Amazing how you can fall in love with the desert and right out again when it blows;

> Amazing how San Francisco can stay so beautiful (Baghdad by the Sea) so exciting, year after year;

> Amazing how hard it is not to gamble when in Vegas to see the shows;

> Amazing how the ocean temperature always seems to drop each time we go to the beach;

Amazing how much everyone likes to receive letters but hates to write them;

Amazing that my tennis game hasn't improved in 30 years;

Amazing how the daughters I thought would never learn to swim and breathe at the same time can now whip me smartly in a sprint;

Amazing how much we miss friends and relatives in the East at Christmastime;

and amazing we weren't all blown off the face of the map this year!

We're still trying to furnish the new four-bedroom casa we bought two years ago in Point Loma, where the sea breezes dissipate the smog and your social standing depends on the magnificence of your view lot, thus how far you can see north to La Jolla, south to Mexico, and west to Hawaii. We are located in the bottom of a canyon with fence-to-fence weeds.

But by puffing to the top of the steep hill two blocks away on our evening strolls, we can rest our orbs on a stretch of the Pacific and pretty Mission Bay and the twinkling lights of San Diego and the silent gray warships lying at anchor in the harbor. Well worth the shin-splints.

We don't drive much. With the furniture it took to furnish this place, we *have* to stay around and sit in it a lot. Sometimes Lovae has us move from room to room on signal.

And don't think that taking care of a lawn 12 months a year out here doesn't cut into the old couch time. Particularly when the little lady pulls a dodge like getting preggers and stops pulling weeds at six months. I come home parched from tennis on Saturday and attack the week's exotic new weed patches and crab grass manifestation before I'm allowed a beer.

Sherrie, our pre-teen, who sleeps 'til noon and is too busy with her hair and records and nails—or too weak from hunger—to do manual labor directs my sweaty efforts from the shaded patio. "You missed a patch over there, Pops." "Hey! That's a flower you're pulling!"

No big vacation again this year. With the weather so glorious here, it seems almost a shame to spend money leaving for any extended period. But in July we told our nosy neighbors we were yachting up at Newport Beach with rich relatives, then high-tailed it down the coast of Mexico to Ensenada and drank two-bit yucca juice and threw firecrackers all night.

Next morning, daughters Sherrie and Debbie and I rented horses (well, they had once been horses) and went riding along the beach. It was beautiful and primitive; the water was green and skies deep blue. Waves rolled in and tugged at the sand beneath us and we drank in the purple mountains and unexplored islands in the off-shore distance. The girls soon raced off into the warm breeze, digging their heels into their steeds, their ponytails flying, until I lost sight of them. My nag didn't apparently understand "giddy-up" in English. I was found at noon, in a cove, fishing with a pin and string for lunch.

The year did see the fulfillment of one of my boyish dreams: To be passed through the gates of MGM studios as a VIP—like I belonged…a hot screenwriter, making an obscene wage.

In reality, last October, it was arranged that I should have lunch with the legendary musical director Busby Berkley—he of first Hollywood musical extravaganzas fame. Now semi-retired, he had visions of doing shows in the Little Theater at our Palm Desert retirement project.

My thoughtful client asked me to check the guy out and bring back a report. Excitedly accepting the assignment, I flew to LA and found myself in a near out-of-body state being admitted with a flourish through the MGM gates.

I found the great Mr. Berkley on the second floor of a nearly vacant, unimposing, gray structure (which had been the former "Writers' Building" where I imagined the wonderful MGM movies of the 1930s and 1940s had been cranked out). After a brief nervous wait, I turned to see the legend emerge—a short, round man with a few strands of gray hair and a rather large, protruding lower lip. He wore both suspenders and a belt—obviously not a fully trusting man.

When he noticed I had been enthusing over some of my favorite star photos hanging in the outer office, he showed no modesty in telling me what a great person he'd been in the old days and how he'd discovered, or given their first roles, to Sinatra, Rooney, Garland, Gable, Turner, etc. Also, that he'd put on the first musical extravaganzas and won Academy Awards and all that stuff.

Eventually, my blood sugar dropping, I was hustled to lunch at the commissary, where I became so involved turning to ogle real actresses and directors, I kept spooning soup in my ear.

After pie á la mode and coffee (we never once talked business), my host decided I was such a true fan, he led me over to the sound stage where they were filming *Dr. Kildare*. I was impressed the way he was greeted with reverence and hugs, from the director to the script girl. I was introduced and studied carefully, as if to see whether I was someone who might have a say in renewing the show for another 13 weeks.

The actors were real crack-ups. After watching them blow five straight scenes, a break was called and we received warm greetings from Richard Chamberlain and Raymond Massey. Maybe it was my imagination, but I felt uncomfortable with the way Richard's gaze held on me.

Outside, I was surprised at the obvious lack of bustle and activity usually seen on movie lots. Busby apologized for this, blaming it on the fact Marlon Brando had used up all the studio's money on *Mutiny on the Bounty*.

The mogul said he, himself, had just been called from retirement to act as assistant director on *Jumbo*, a circus film with Jimmy Durante. He confessed he hated TV because it had put so many old-time movie guys like him out of business as it caught the public's fancy in the late '50s. The times they are a-changing, I kept thinking as I headed back to the airport.

It turned out the "Hollywood touch" didn't fit the profile for our sensitive little community. So we had to reject his proposal.

Now Lovae and I look forward to spending New Year's Eve in San Francisco. Whoopee! Coincides with my agency handling the grand opening of another community for folks in their senior years: Endsville North, you might say.

As a bonus for not cheating at petty cash this year, I have been awarded tickets to the Rose Bowl Game, where I'll probably have a vascular episode (not a sexual remark) if Wisconsin doesn't win, Big Ten fan that I still am! And if the little mother gets too excited watching the Badgers battle the Trojans, she may give birth before 100,000 cheering fans.

She's due in mid-January, according to a doctor I pay an annuity to for guessing. I asked him if there was any reason I have to be in the delivery room while my wife is in labor. He said, "Not unless the words 'alimony' and 'child support' mean anything to you."

Hope Santa's real good to you, and may your liquor bills be excused.

I close with this inspirational thought for the New Year: "If you smile when nobody else is around, you really mean it." Or are demented.

Heigh Ho, Santa's Helpers!

1964

I'd rather stick evergreen needles up my nose than attend another holiday office party. Wound up in Mexico smuggling some kind of addictive chocolate liquor back across the border after the last one. But so far, I haven't lost any clients—and am still allowed in the house.

So here we are a week before Santa loads up, and I haven't penned a year-end "review of a mad writer" to friends and relatives. My apologies to all five of you.

Lovae and I've been cruising the area's first regional shopping center, College Grove, which I helped with its grand opening a while back. Twenty-some new stores—eager to share your Christmas bonus. Thousands of people milling about in shorts and sandals. But wearing a guarded smile. They know this dream-like life can last just so long before the Big Shake comes!

With four kiddies now in our household, we had a screamingly lively year. We didn't want to miss a minute of it, so Lovae locked up the prescription drugs.

We've cut down on our trips to the Emergency Room, because little mother could probably qualify as an RN herself now. She can wrap a sprain in nothing flat, set a broken finger and stem the flow of blood before I start seeing black spots. Then, when she isn't in the laundry room, she's the head chef and short-order cook. We give her a break and eat out some weekends. Nice the kids think McDonald's is a four-star restaurant.

Our new shortstop, Gary, will be two in just a month. These 9-pound boys Lovae produces don't stay babies long. Gary was walking and trying to fix his own oatmeal at seven months. Lovae's down to 101 pounds attempting to keep up with him. Lifting kids and furniture all these years has given her amazing upper-body strength, though. She could raise a car off an accident victim.

I don't believe I told you that just before Gary's birth last year, I needed to be in Palm Springs on business. Our O.B. assured us the baby's arrival was a week away. Lovae's best friend and neighbor, Marie Dunphy, didn't approve at all of my leaving, no doubt spotting the golf clubs in the car.

Sure enough, the little mother went into labor early the second morning of my absence. Marie rushed her to the hospital and sent word for me to hustle back to San Diego. Upon hearing this early morning news, I raced through a driving rain-storm in the mountains, down the freeway at 85 mph and screeched into the hospital parking lot. Marie was just heading for her car. "Hey, Marie!" I yelled out, "How's Lovae?"

"Well, Bill, you have a baby *boy*," she announced curtly. "I counted and he has 10 fingers and 10 toes. Now you can go back to your Palm Springs!"

Our two teenie-bopper girls enjoy playing "mother" and holding the little tyke, though they become invisible at diaper-changing time.

Both girls are right up there in their class (not just in height). I don't know how they do it with a phone pressed to their ears, cutting off the blood supply to the brain while doing homework, with some rock musician hurting himself on the radio at the decibel level of a Boeing B-25.

Our lissome youngest, Deborah, is faster than her male classmates, so had to tank it in track meets before she could procure a date offer.

With the baby taking over my den, I'm doing my writing on an ironing board in the kitchen. But it may have changed my luck. I sold a second short story to a men's magazine! We celebrated on the meager proceeds for two weeks. But I've been directed to hide copies of the racy publication from the children 'til they're 18.

You probably read about our torrential rains last spring. Well, it nailed us in a fun surprise. Our house was flooded. Not bad…I can soggily report. But you haven't lived until you've been pulled naked out of the morning shower by a teenager who shouts: "Oh, daddy, come see this absolutely crazy water seeping into our family room from the back yard!"

So now dig the scene: I'm on all fours, with a three-Anacin headache, mopping up a muddy torrent in my heavily mortgaged family room, and the youngest girl is standing there yelling: "The ark is sinking, the ark is sinking…"

But moments later, the black skies suddenly lifted and the backyard water (from a storm drain that backed up in the canyon) started to recede as we watched in awe. We quick-dried the rug. It shrank 3 inches on each side, turning a barf brown.

In spite of these shocks that life holds in store for each of us, I still have all my hair and porcelain-filled teeth. And I almost never show resentment that Lovae, my 34-year-old fairy princess, could pass for 20 (she was carded at a club the other night, while I was passed right through).

She shows none of the ravages of age—probably a combination of good genes and the fact that she enjoys the typical suburban conveniences of a modern housewife when she's not in the maternity ward. Like she has a new GE dishwasher, two televisions and a Mexican maid who illegally crosses the border to rearrange the dust every other Friday. Gives Lovae time to fertilize her flowers and fruit trees. (She's growing oranges as big as basketballs!)

Still, like most women, she wants more. Next year, she has demanded we go someplace other than Disneyland on vacation. Fortunately, I have connections at Knotts Berry Farm.

This summer, I took her to the track for the first time to "play the ponies," as we insiders say. One of my clients is the famous Del Mar Race Track, "Where the Turf Meets the Surf," founded by Bing Crosby and Pat O'Brien.

We were seated near the finish line at a table in the Turf Club, where we gawked at the likes of J. Edgar Hoover, Jimmy Durante, Ann Margaret, Harry James, Betty Grable, and Vince Edwards, *Ben Casey*.

While standing in line, fingering a five and trying to figure out how to properly say I wanted to put $2 on number 3 and $3 on number 2, a race track tout behind me says to his partner, "Geez, Eddie, I hope I break even today. I could use the money."

To continue with the name-dropping, last winter I was invited to go on a freebie long-weekend ski trip with Jack Kemp, the ex-Chargers quarterback. I had interviewed him in '62 for a piece I wrote for the AFL All-Star Game souvenir magazine. This turned into a friendship, and we socialized with Jack and Joanne on several occasions. Jack once brought over his autographed photo for daughter Debbie, who was quite madly in love with him, and had to be revived when Jack entered her bedroom to present his surprise gift.

Anyway, Jack and I arrived by bus at Mammoth in a blizzard and 60 inches of "new powder" (as we say on the slopes). The next morning, while I practiced falling on the bunny slopes, Jack almost bought the farm. He had headed for a forbidden area to try a virgin run from the top. He crashed at mach speed, plunging headfirst into about 7 feet of snow. Unable to extricate himself, he's on his last breath in this deserted area—when another speed demon skis down behind him, spots Jack's skis sticking up and stops to pull him out!

When we met for coffee an hour later, I innocently asked Jack why his complexion was such a funny reddish-purple. He threw pieces of donut at me.

San Diego has a new tourist attraction, SeaWorld, which opened in March. I quietly went for an interview late last year, feeling it's time to look for something outside the agency business. Over 100 disillusioned citizens applied, and I made the cut to the last five—but lost out.

Maybe just as well. The place, mainly a big aquarium with several dolphin or sea lion shows, is located on 22 acres of former mud flats in nearby Mission Bay. It'll be fortunate to survive. After all, we have Marineland an hour's hop to the north. And no attraction beats our knock-out zoo!

Speaking of Mission Bay, Lovae and I nearly crippled ourselves in it with an attempt to stay up on water skis last summer when our heads must have had too much sun. Lovae fell on the second attempt and couldn't let go of the handle. She had bruises on her thighs that didn't disappear until Thanksgiving.

I made it up on the third attempt and must have skied a mile in somewhat of a petrified state—afraid to let go. For three days after, I walked around work like Groucho Marx. Think we'll stick to badminton in the back yard for family recreation.

Those are the publishable highlights of our year. Let us hear about yours.

Hope you have a jolly, merry, fun Christmas and will hoist one to us…as we will to you.

In the New Year remember: "Misers are no fun to live with, but they make great ancestors."

A Merry Hello! 1966

It's late Sunday evening and Lovae's locked in our bedroom wrapping presents, while Gary tries to pick the lock. Craig has the FBI shooting it out with the bad guys on TV, and the sound clashes slightly with the wailing from the rock station which emanates from Debbie's bedroom, where she's finishing a painting that would startle Dali. Sherrie is out in the garage hollering for her mother to come help repair something, since it's common knowledge in the neighborhood that her father is "fix-it" handicapped.

I have to admit, I'm pretty much useless once you get past the hammer. But Lovae's a whiz at repairing and constructing stuff. I try to help—like I hold the board while she saws. I'd get her a tool belt this year if they had one in a petite size. I'm still trying to live down putting Craig's new bike together last Christmas with the pedals on inside-out.

So—just another cacophonous day in Paradise as we prepare for Santa's drop-in visit. I'm trying hard to get pumped up for Christmas, but just can't get the yuletide juices going.

I awoke early, my youngest—who suffers from insomnia about the time the sun breaks over England—having discovered how to work the broken tape recorder, which had some 25 minutes of either a New Year's party, or a monster chase from the *Lost in Space* show. After I ripped the batteries from the machine, I clutched the child to my breast, and carted him to the galley for breakfast while the wife slept off yesterday's shopping hangover. It wasn't bacon and eggs (I don't cook either), but the little fella quaffed two boxes of cereal and three powdered donuts like he'd just come off two weeks' solitary confinement.

The sun boosted the morning temperature to an un-Christmas-like 75 degrees, so the newest offspring and I scooted up to the high school track as part of my fitness program, which I hope will help me reach 50 without a pacemaker. (Lovae says the only thing more boring than sickness is fitness.)

Gary and I played a little handball, until I pulled something I didn't even know I had, then limped home to catch the Chargers on TV. The Chargers, it turns out, couldn't catch a cold. By sundown, I had to be medicated. And it was time to go pick up a few decorations and some wax for Sherrie's phantom mustache and find the perfect tree.

I expended a hundred bucks and couldn't find a suitable tree, despite an hour spent tracking around in the mud by the light of a cold moon and taking a few branches in the orbs during close inspection. "Oh, look at this big one back here, Daddy—oops!" *Yowee!*

So no tree yet and the kids aren't speaking. And I was sitting here staring at the bills and the party invitations, which will cause me to be ill on certain mornings of the holidays, and I thought, heck, why not cheer up and write you?

So you see, said the Grinch, there is some good comes from all the pre-Christmas chaos.

First, many have asked about my throwing in with the monkeys last year. Well, three things are destined to remain a mystery. The lost continent of Atlantis, the extinction of the dinosaurs, and how I wound up in a zoo.

Suffice it to say, I was only kidding when I filled out a zoological society application at a friend's urging. But after a couple of unproductive interviews, in which I determined it might be better to stay with the ulcer-producing agency business, I was called in and named the new publicist for the San Diego Zoo. (Maybe the personnel guy liked my after-shave lotion!)

Yeah, the kid from Iowa, once allergic to cats and afraid of tall dogs, is a press agent for 5,000 beasties. I beat out 137 housewives, retired military officers, and alcoholic newsmen for the coveted position.

While I'm intrigued and stimulated by this new wild world, I always check the ground behind me when passing the snake house. But truth be known, folks, I may have found my niche. I love the place and enjoy pumping out the stories and wild photos. Every time you pick up a paper or turn on the TV this year, seems we're there. One curator said he's noticed a real pick-up in the zoo's press coverage (he also imbibes a bit).

The year-long celebration of the great zoo's 50th birthday was a smashing success and kept us hopping for weeks. During the time we had seminars with animal experts from all over the world, Lovae also worked at the headquarters hotel. We met such luminaries as Jane Goodall, the chimp lady, and Ian Player (golfer Gary's brother), who is chief conservator of Zululand.

Last month, I racked up a *Life Magazine* plant—with the birth of the first Proboscis Monkey in a zoo (father "Pinocchio" has a hilarious 3-inch-long nose).

Made national news, myself, when I was scratched by a lion. But it was just a few scratches by a cub, Brian Lion, until AP played it for serious. "Zoo PR Man Clawed by a Lion…"

Our world-famous menagerie draws over 2.5 million gawkers a year, who flock in with their plaid shorts and white legs and drop wrappers and popcorn boxes all over the well-kept grounds. We're the second largest tourist attraction in the West and some days outdraw Disney. Which doesn't seem to bother Walt in the least.

What's kinda groovy is that I get to work almost every week with people from MGM or Fox, LA television guys, or NY crews here to shoot commercials. Plus, I'm coordinating producer of our own *Zoorama*, a widely syndicated TV show (which means I type up the meeting notes, and get ice cream for the monkeys or peanuts for the elephants when it's their time on camera).

The keepers are a kick to be around and have lots of stories. One, an ex-circus type, told me a frustrated visitor called him over one day to the chimpanzee cages where the occupants were busily mating. The man said, "We're trying to take photos—do you think if I threw them some peanuts, they'd stop that?"

The keeper said he shook his head and replied, "I don't know, sir…would you?"

Well, I should go string up the house lights and surprise Lovae (so she and the kids don't have to do it). But why risk a broken clavicle and add to wifey's traditional pre-Christmas tizzy. I'll tack up a wreath on the door tomorrow and maybe hang a few plastic icicles on the palm trees to help me get into the spirit of the season.

Then I have the humbling task of deciding which gift my wonderful, hard-to-fit, petite wife will take back to which store the day after she opens it and holds it up as she would a dead rabbit. "Nice, honey. *Where'd* you find this?"

Looking forward with glee to hearing from you. Best wishes from all of us.

Here's an old African proverb to ponder in 1967: "There are 40 kinds of lunacy, but only one kind of common sense."

Joyous Greetings!

"*Chui!*" our native driver whispered excitedly, pointing to a nearby clump of trees in Tanzania's famous Serengeti National Park.

"Anyone who can find their way to the pet store and back knows that 'chui' in Swahili means 'leopard,'" the lady riding behind me snapped when I asked.

In the ensuing excitement, I rolled up my wife's hair in the van window and dropped my $300 borrowed Mamiya camera with built-in exposure meter and 210-mm telephoto lens. A solitary animal whose numbers are swiftly diminishing, you don't often find leopard on camera safari, our tour leader announced as she pridefully passed the hat for tips.

In September, I was named the San Diego Zoo's rep for the annual safari to East Africa. Lovae packed enough clothes for all touring members and came along for the ride.

So there we were, with 18 others, in the middle of Tanzania after spending the previous night in Seronera Camp, headquarters for the 5,700-square-mile game preserve. The park is home to the world's greatest population of wild animals, if you could believe

31

the booklet a native with an empty Budweiser can embedded in his ear lobe had sold me at the park's entrance.

Since 1920, my literature pointed out, the camp had been HQ for white hunters seeking lion, and for Hollywood crews shooting movies and practicing their Tarzan yells. But time and indoor plumbing had passed it by. The quarters were old and musty. Food was bland to barfy. I hadn't seen a mosquito yet in Africa, but dingy mosquito netting hung over our beds. I tried sleeping with one eye open, listening for tsetse fly sounds. But I must have dozed off, exhausted as I was after eight hours of careening over Africa's non-roads that day.

Around midnight, my wife ripped me from my lumpy bunk to see the "cute" animal outside our window. I stuck my head out— and there in the moon-light, came eye-ball-to-eye-ball with a snorting bull African buffalo, slobbering and munching up our lawn. I slammed the window and pulled the covers over my head, half-anticipating his charge through the thin walls when he ran out of grass.

So it was with something less than boyish enthusiasm that I arose to a chilly sun, shaved in a frosty basin of water, nibbled at a breakfast of eggs and wart hog (I saw one chicken in Africa but we always had eggs!) then piled into the six-passenger bus for the morning "hunt."

Our keen-eyed guides had flushed out several hyena and a family of cheetah, when we came upon the rare find—a leopard flaked out half-way up in the branches of a baron tree.

We joined three other VW buses under the tree and hurriedly began photographing the zonked-out female before she awoke. But we need not have been concerned. The sleek feline remained motionless, eyes shut, her pose ridiculous.

"She is hunting," our native driver whispered. I looked again. She was sprawled languidly over three limbs, her legs and tail dangling below, looking like the "morning after." Sure she is, I thought. And you've been nipping. That cat's asleep.

In the ensuing 10 minutes, while we quietly clicked away, nine other safari buses and land rovers roared in from different directions and jockeyed noisily for position. It looked for a minute like we were back at Fifth and Broadway in the five o'clock traffic.

Just as we were convinced the hundred-pound cat would snooze away the day, she pried one eye open. Then the other. Then she yawned hugely and was awake—up and alert.

A chill traveled the length of my spine, and made a return trip, as the African killer gazed down at me, thick paws outstretched in a Sphinx-like pose, green eyes in a penetrating gaze. She was so close I could see the gold flecks around the pupils of her eyes in my lens.

Seemingly unconcerned by our presence (animals in the game reserves appear to know shooting is not allowed), the female suddenly tensed and fixed her eye on a young Thompson's gazelle grazing in our direction. "See, out there—she is hunting," our driver-guide whispered, again. And now, of course, his carload of couch potatoes had to admit he was right.

For 20 minutes the leopard crouched and watched. When the little antelope finally moved downwind, *chui* left the tree in a lightning movement, like someone had rung the dinner bell. In the next 10 minutes, stalking with ears laid back, head low, she closed the 50-yard gap between her and her unsuspecting prey. When she was almost within sprinting distance, engines behind her started, vehicles edging closer, so their ga-ga occupants could photograph the anticipated kill. But the gazelle, startled by the 13 motors coming to life, bounded off to safety.

The disappointed stalker settled for a confused African hare that jumped up in front of her in the short, brown grass. And didn't we all feel guilty when we discovered our leopard mom had been hunting to feed her three cubs, hidden in a thicket a quarter-of-a-mile away.

I felt so bad, it took about four gins to return my sunny disposition that evening around the camp-fire. We chatted with the native drivers, who pointed out that if it weren't for the dollars spent by spoiled tourists like us on safari, the parks couldn't stay open, and the vanishing herds would be further decimated by natives and hunters. (Amazing fact: 70 percent of the population of Tanzania have never seen a lion, elephant, or buffalo!)

There were so many highlights to remember about Africa as I sit here, trying to get the lyrics of "White Christmas" out of my head for a minute. Uganda, for example, where we began our three-week trek, a lush, green beauty, with its manicured tea fields and the natives' shiny black faces and wide, toothy grins, won our collective hearts. I slipped Kleenex to three of the single women on our tour as we prepared to leave magical Uganda's friendly borders. Then they sat down and wept, knowing a return trip might never be in the books. (Idi Amin, the despot!)

The ride to Simliki Lodge on the main road to the Belgian Congo was the *roughest* of the whole trip (a specially-built VW bus like ours lasts only 12,000 miles on those pot-holed roads…the human spine less).

And maybe the two nights in a no-water, no-electricity tent camp, 30 miles from the Pygmies, with lions prowling within 50 yards, may go down as one of our great outdoor adventures. (One a lifetime, please.) The first night we were so damned excited about the lions, we couldn't wait to crash in our sacks and listen for them to wander near. About midnight I came to and heard one roaring. I called to Lovae. She finally came to, rose up and listened. "Go back to sleep," she said tiredly, "it's just Dr. Hubbs in the next tent snoring."

Certainly showering by pulling a rope on a water barrel set in a tree was more primitive than our travel brochure had led us to believe. Particularly on a frosty morn following a horizontal rain that blew at least one tent down. And sharing the Rent-A-John with three lizards and a giant beetle was closer to nature than I ever got at Little League.

Oddly, the food served under a decorative shed-like structure was delicious and not exotic (only once did we have zebra and several times their wonderful lake fish).

Some of you will have difficulty envisioning me helping push a stuck safari bus out of the shoe-top-deep mud on our first lion hunt. But the kid from Iowa was right in there, working on a hernia.

Good grief! Was it only three months ago that I boated up the Nile to Murchison Falls, snapping photos at only two arm-lengths from pop-eyed hippos and mean-toothed crocs? One matronly lady seated in front of us jumped up and said: "I'm surprised they let our boat get this close to these crocodiles, they're so dangerous."

Some wag called out: "They're mechanical—like at Disneyland."

The gal plopped back down, saying: "Oh, I'm so disappointed. I thought they'd be real here in Africa."

Later, we sipped Waragi gin (Ugandan 70 proof) on the patio at Paraa Lodge while watching the native dancers. Soon a hyena, and finally an elephant, tippy-toed up on the lawn for a look-see. I resisted offering a potato chip.

Was it just October or two years ago that I saw 50,000 Uganda Kob, flushed out our first lioness, and had to buy a round of drinks after being the Big Bwana who spotted a white rhino taking a private mud bath in the brush at Murchison?

I don't know now—time and my memory stretch out like the vast African sky.

After my usual futile attempts at Christmas shopping and finding a tree to please the kids, I could stand a little R & R at the swank Nairobi Hilton where we stayed on different occasions to get our wind (we covered 3,000 miles of East Africa by ground transportation—and our total trip, including stops in Rome and London—totaled 33,000 miles).

We first left Nairobi one morning on a two-hour drive through Kikuyland and had lunch at the Aberdare Country Club, then piled into Land Rovers for an 11-mile ride up the forest road to the secluded ARK (built upon pilings) in the company of an armed guard.

Our wide-eyed group silently crossed a draw-bridge, taken up at 4:00 P.M. so no one could come or leave, and waited in a glassed-in viewing room. As promised, darkness brought elephant and buffalo, rhino and bushbuck to sample the salt lick below our window.

Though a fire roared in the fireplace—with me throwing furniture on—we still wrapped in a blanket to keep from freezing our whatchamacallits at 7,600 feet in the Aberdares, the eastern wall of the Great Rift Valley. In the distance Satina and Kinangop touched clouds at 13,000 feet. We sacked in with hot water bottles! About 3:00 A.M., I borrowed Lovae's.

Our next run out of Nairobi (a colorful, bustling capital city of Kenya with some 300,000 Western-looking citizens) took us into Masai country where we soon got stuck in 2-foot dust! Late in the day, we stopped for the night in the beautifully constructed Keekorok Lodge, remote from the established safari route, a jewel in an area seemingly unmolested by civilization.

The next morning's drive took us into the Serengeti, which seems to be the Africa one expects to see. (Was it here or Murchison that our Australian lady-friend from Hawaii misunderstood the driver calling out a bird in the distance named a Kori Bustard, and said "I say, could he possibly have said that bird is a horny bah-stard?") We loved her and felt for her when she was the first to spot a giraffe, which she filmed frantically, then cried when she found she had the lense cover on!

The Ngorongoro Crater—our lodge perched 2,000 feet up on the rim—just might be one of the world's top 10 sights. The primitive ride down has to rank among the top three most sobering experiences. The food in the Lodge was worth the price of the whole trip. My pictures of the lions mating are worth the price of coming to California to see.

A side trip to Olduvai Gorge turned me on, as it is the site of Dr. Leakey's discoveries of earliest man. *Zinjanthropus*, which I believe his wife discovered while trying to bury the garbage one night, is said to be 1,750,000 years old. I felt younger than I've ever felt that day.

A fitting climax to the trip was another tent camp, Amboseli, at the base of Mt. Kilimanjaro. Lovae and I sat around a blazing evening fire and drank toasts to Hemingway and Ruark, a couple of fair writers who stayed in camp some time before we discovered it.

An exciting morning drive in search of game was topped by a black rhino and her young charging our particular VW bus. I stuck my head out the top of the vehicle and snapped several thrilling shots of a four-foot horn about to impale us—just before banging my crazy bone and screaming to our grinning driver: "Faster!"

Lovae said it was similar to someone trying to film their own death.

We left Africa with mixed feelings—eager to return to home base, but knowing we had only seen a small part of this hypnotically-interesting maze of countries. Two of our band are going back to Kenya to live and work next year.

The flights to London—then to San Diego—took so long I had to ask if Nixon was still president when we landed. Our orphaned children, looking thinner, greeted us with screeches and hugs and went through our luggage for food.

Our house was still in one piece. Is there anything that looks better after three weeks on another continent than your own home? The cracked back door and the broken pictures were caused, we were told, by a small earthquake, unreported anywhere but our neighborhood. Sure…and we believe our kids could sell earmuffs in the Congo.

Anyway, we didn't sweat the small stuff. We fell into bed and hoped to sleep for about a week. Unfortunately, I had been missed at work, according to an early morning call the next day.

Now we're nowhere near ready for Santa, so must go to the mall and see if we can spend an hour with the last hundred we didn't fork out on Masai spears and cowhide shields.

I'll tell you more about our adventure next year. Unless you make the mistake of coming to see us—then we'll show you 600 color slides!

Hope you are well and planning much fun for the holidays.

In the coming year remember: "The man who rows the boat doesn't have time to rock it."

Cheers and Glad Tidings!

I was just sitting here staring vacantly at the Christmas bills, trying to come up with a snappy opening for the holiday letter. A toy, it says, for $49.50. When I was 10, that would have bought out Lindsey's candy counter, put me in the Saturday movies for nine months and taken my Uncle Mark off relief.

The bill was for one of nine toys purchased for the youngest heir. "How can we afford this?" I questioned. "I haven't sold the book yet!"

"But he's promised to cut the grass until he's in junior high," my dark-eyed beauty bribed. "Just write your letter and forget the bills. A little humor might help people forget theirs."

There is nothing humorous about the Arabs cutting off our oil supply and crippling attendance for my new employer, SeaWorld. Our visitors need lots of gas to drive their autos here to see our talented whales and dolphins and seals and a bazillion fish, all of which cost obscene amounts of money to keep. (You ever seen the grocery bill for a 4-ton orca?)

As a result, we've had to cut our budgets, several members of the staff and lunches.

SeaWorld stock is down 11 points. Another five and mine will have only curiosity value.

Kind of ironic that I'm PR director for the very place most of us (experts?) felt could not compete in the crowded Southern California tourist attraction market. But once they brought in a killer whale and taught it not to eat the trainers, attendance zoomed. Most people come, I suspect, to see whether the killers *will* chomp on the trainers. (Same reason millions go to the Indianapolis 500—hoping not just to watch the cars go round-and-round, but to see a crash!)

The park got its first national recognition when Hugh Downs rode Shamu for a segment on the *Today* show around 1967. Also, millions saw a comical bunch of SeaWorld–trained penguins roller-skate on *The Jack Benny Show*. Quite a few decided to come see for themselves. That's how that works.

I left the zoo last year, for those of you who weren't paying attention, right after holding the grand opening for the Wild Animal Park. We planned the official late afternoon ceremonies for six months. The director, Dr. Schroeder, warned me to go over every detail twice to preclude any chance of a hitch occurring. I did and all went beautifully—almost to the end. When the mayor rose from the outdoor banquet table to speak, the automatic sprinklers went on.

A certain amount of shrieking and diving for cover followed among the distinguished guests, I recall painfully. They had to catch me down by the hyenas to tell me it wasn't my fault, and I could come back and have din-din. (I believe it was the head gardener who was fired.)

I left my wild job with the monkeys for the proverbial "new challenge" and a few pesos more in the monthly check. SeaWorld officials interviewed me privately in June for the second time, offering me goodies to help them jump-start attendance, same as they felt I had for the zoo (mainly by establishing an ambassador position, hiring Joan Embery to fill it and getting her on *The Tonight Show* with Johnny Carson).

And now, to save energy, we've had to cut back the hours our goliath "Christmas tree" will be lit. We torch it up Saturday night in a gala pageant with bands and festivities. Billed modestly as California's tallest at 320 feet, it consists of 2,000 lights strung from our American Airlines Flagship Tower (ride). We had to cancel the 100-boat parade, so I was hard-pressed to come up with a gimmick to amuse the jaded media. But I poured a little Smirnoff and settled for a Santa flying in at 8:00 P.M. on a Delta-wing kite with red and green flares smoking. That'll blow some minds. And if our dare-devil crashes, I'll be assigned to the bait barge!

Otherwise, we did some interesting TV bits in the park during '73. Like a couple Lloyd Bridges (Sea Hunt) specials, two with Bill Daley (Bob Newhart's neighbor in the Saturday night winner), Howard Cosell, Chuck Conners, and a wild show called *The Thrill Seekers* (second part should run this month). Also, I have one of the whale riders due on *What's My Line?* and we won an Emmy for a show I had nothing to do with called *Gigi Goes Home*, concerning the return to the sea of a 27-foot gray whale that nearly broke us by eating 2,400 pounds of fish a day while on display (at a cost of $100,000 a year).

My personal big thrill of the year, I guess, was taking Astronaut Eugene Cernan (last man to walk on the moon) around the park one day with his daughter. We had a high dive show as an added feature at the Dolphin Lagoon. At dusk, we sat tensely while a muscled young diver began a slow, dramatic climb to a drum roll up toward the 70-foot top of the ladder. Cernan, holding his nervous child's hand, whispered to me: "Is he going to the top and dive off?" I nodded grimly. The famed astronaut let out some air and said: "Boy, you'd never get me up there!"

I later had him autograph a photo of us posing with a dolphin. Which I subsequently spilled coffee on.

Otherwise, the usual hair-graying year with the family. I was called to the hospital emergency room when my little guy imbedded a fishhook in his hand, my eldest boy totaled our Subaru in a thrilling, but illegal, lefthand turn, and number-two daughter was in a flaming car accident on one of California's famous freeways, in which she suffered slight back and leg juries. She is still pretty and mobile and about to collect $5,000, of which her parents are claiming $2,000 for mental anguish.

Lovae, our full-time chef, was catatonic for some weeks after all this, so we sent her to Hawaii for a month with her mother and sister, Hazel Dawn. She returned in October, tanned and rested and relaxed for the first time in ages. Her nervous tic didn't return for 72 hours.

The big news, of course, was that Sherrie made us grandparents in April! Sort of destroyed your image of me as 29, didn't it? But Angela Tiffany is a keeper. I get kind of silly when speaking of this little bundle with the devastating smile.

One day, for example, a PR friend arranged for Sherrie and my mother to go up on the Goodyear Blimp. I waited below, amusing Angela. Soon an elderly couple stopped and said: "What a perfectly adorable daughter you have, sir." I didn't bother to explain that I was the grandfather. Mainly, because I still can't believe it. I wish I could say she looked a lot like me. But I'm grayer...

I did have my moment this year, however. I managed my little tiger's team to the Major League baseball championship. After eight years, we finally landed a first again. My pitching elbow will never be the same, and I've been resting and treating it for six months. The kid stopped taking my batting instructions and wound up hitting .440, much to the surprise of me and five other managers. I didn't know how much a first-place win pleased him until I saw him shower with his trophy.

Also had the satisfaction of seeing our high school win the county baseball championship. Eight of the starting nine were kids who played for me or were in our league a few years back.

Gary entered Pop Warner football, but I didn't coach. He was fullback and safety in a fairly disastrous season. It sort of began and ended when he carried the ball for the first time, sprinting 78 yards for a touchdown, and it was called back.

But his team was more interesting than the Chargers! We gave up on those bandits for the first time in a dozen years and boycotted several games. Previously we had missed only two games since 1961—one while we were in Africa and one when Gary threw up down my neck while we were speeding to the stadium. I later attended the awards luncheon with a phony smile as we presented our Willie the Walrus award for the best lineman to Russ Washington. And I can't even say: "Wait'll next year." It's criminal what they've done to that team.

Hard to believe the three-year-old son I drove out here 15 years ago will graduate in June and be heading for college. His best grade is in surfing! But he's a fine specimen, taller now than his dad and lovin' it, and making a few bucks as a bus boy in a steak house.

No exotic trips this year for SeaWorld—tho some of the staff went to Japan, Mexico City, Alaska and Antarctica. My reward was a trip to *Houston* for the national conference of the American Association of Zoological Parks and Aquariums. Saw a lot of old zoo friends…and met Marlin Perkins for the first time. Looked like himself…

Oh, yes. I helped the boss put on a political benefit at our restaurant with Les Brown's band, Rosemary Clooney, and Larry Storch. Raised $30,000 and acquired the attention of the grand jury for some minor fund-raising violations.

If we don't get put in the slammer, I will probably travel to Florida for the formal opening of SeaWorld number 3, which is located next to Disney World.

That's all, folks! Why not plan to honor us with your presence in 1974?

Hope you have a wildly wonderful holiday! And remember Mark Twain's words: "Get your facts first, and then you can distort them as much as you please."

Greetings From
Our House to Yours!

So, here we are again after another perfectly marvy year.

I'm $894 in debt and haven't bought a present yet, and Lovae said I should sit down and write something funny *tonight*, or we'll have to send the letter with our Valentines.

Funny, hmm? Well, it wasn't so funny when she caused my hair to go gray right down the middle. She had a breast cyst removed in March. Thankfully, it was benign. Debbie's boy friend, a former catcher for the Dodgers, helped me home after Lovae's surgery. We both OD'd on tomato juice and Galliano, but recovered in time to bring her home for the spring planting.

She's been morose about the plantings, however. The tsetse fly some nosy agriculture inspector found in our orange tree was an isolated one, and now that the orange tree is dead, there probably won't be any repeated visits from tsetse flies.

The boys have grown fantastically. Craig took his first full-time job at the age of 29 (well, it seems like it). He's a plumber's apprentice. He had to do something. The invention he'd been working on for a year was found to be already patented. However, his summer garden was a great success. Nobody died from the mushrooms he planted, and I'm sure we're all better off from the purge. The neighbors are friendly and won't sue.

Gary and I spent half the year in baseball. He broke his hand in mid-season. His batting average was .580, highest in the league's 20 years, but of course it was six games shy of a full season. Still, he was named an All-Star. We worked 39 days and figured to go to Williamsport this time. We lost our first game in extra innings and Gary struck out on a pitch that bounced in front of the plate. That didn't hurt as much as the two scouts who got up and left the stands. Gary doesn't take the losses as hard as I do. He locks himself in this room and does Zen.

My mom is fine, enjoying the rain and cold we had most of the weird weather year. She keeps asking why she left Iowa. She has a cozy apartment several blocks up the hill from us. Her fall over the phone cord at least keeps her inside away from the damp outdoors.

I started my third year as a grandfather in March. There are no courses on how to act, so I'm still not handling it too well. I've taught the child to call me daddy when we're out. Angie has intelligent blue eyes, is quick on the uptake and knows how to work me for trips to SeaWorld and the Wild Animal Park. Her really big dream, she has confided, is to sleep one night with the gorillas. (I trust that has no deep significance.)

I see by my whale calendar that April was the month of my big business trip this year—to our park in Ohio. I pow-wowed with our public relations agency reps from Pittsburgh, Toledo and LA on plans for opening the new $1 million Cap'n Kids World within the summer park. We later flew several of the Walton kids out for the occasion.

The whole opening day bombed, I stayed in a motel in Chagrin Falls and couldn't get a baked potato with my catfish at 9:00 P.M. because the kitchen was closed. Next morning, I waded through the snow, drove to Cleveland and had tears in my eyes, so happy was I to land in San Diego, where we had only a light smog alert.

In May, my brother Mark, now in the flower business in Miami (after nine years with our state department trying to stop cocaine shipments from South America to the United States), wrote that he'd made a killing Mother's Day. In June, he called again to say he'd had another big month and was threatened by the Mafia for transporting flowers into Canada—their territory.

I told him, "Listen, kid, don't let them bluff you. You're entitled to your cut of the pie. Don't believe all that Godfather jazz in the movies." But he pulled out of Canada a few weeks later after he found a wreath in the shape of a horse's-head in his bed one morning.

In June, our trip to the desert was cut short by heavy moisture, but it was time to come home anyway because the Coleman stove blew up. Actually, we had a lively get-together with our former Africa traveling companions. We tippled a few and told lies around the fire all night, pretending we were back at Kilimanjaro with the ghost of Hemingway.

My daughters may have gotten more beautiful, if I may say so without sounding like a braggart. (As my boss growls whenever he sees them: "Thank God they look like their mother!") Sherrie is still separated and happily dating several different guys. She just moved into her own apartment with a killer view.

Deb has modeled for the bank where she is employed. She's featured in a full-page color shot in their annual report. A good-looking stud in her office seems to have noticed and is spiriting her away on a big ski trip to Colorado in January. This is the first year we've given her thermal underwear for Christmas.

A bloodless coup occurred in my office, if we must speak of offices. I had to fire my assistant, my photographer quit to join our ex-president at Seven Seas of Texas, and I helped my secretary make up her mind to leave for a job where she would only have to do one thing at a time. My new secretary was named by *Redbook* magazine as one of the 20 most beautiful women in Arizona a while back, and who cares if she can't type? (Besides Lovae!)

At the end of August, I spent two weeks in my den, whanging away at the book. It's really good—too bad I can't finish it. Lovae got to looking a little wild-eyed (she has to feed me six times a day on the hypoglycemia diet), so we booked passage to Hawaii in September. What a fine, relaxing time we had (Maui was my favorite and I shall return). Our Hilton friends here had us marked VIP at the hotels and Western upgraded us to first class, so we were treated like we had money. Even played tourist and watched them shoot *Hawaii Five-O* on the beach one day. James MacArthur is short.

If you watched Monday night football in October, you saw Howard plug Shamu and the girl who was to ride him on his Saturday night show. It was estimated by my boss that the free plugs we pulled off that week, and the 25 million audience who watched SeaWorld that Saturday night was worth $500,000. I bought a new disposal with my bonus.

All and all, it was the busiest and most successful year ever for the big fish show. Each of our parks set records in attendance. We even paid our first dividend and have an NBC special coming up in mid-January. The producer told me that he has filmed shows all over the world and that the Yankee Doodle Whale is the finest animal act he has ever seen!

Then there was the furor caused, as you may know, by our display of the great white shark in late summer. I have never personally been involved with anything that caused the press reaction this did. For example, the staff and I did over 70 radio interviews in five days. Had calls into the evening for weeks and were on every program in LA, Mike Douglas, etc. All because of that crazy movie, *Jaws!* Did we luck out…and cash in.

Otherwise, I served as president of the Mission Bay Lessees Association, was 1st VP of the Press Club, and accepted a board position with Starlight Musicals just before an officer of that group was indicted on 22 counts of fraud, embezzlement, etc.

I leave you with these words of inspiration for what we hope is a successful New Year: "Happiness is an agreeable sensation arising from contemplating the misery of another."

Happy
Santa...

Didn't we just go through the Ho, Ho, Ho bit a few months ago?

Here I am, late again! Just because I didn't get anything done until Christmas eve in 1948, does that mean I won't ever catch up the rest of my life?

Guess Santa has a way of sneaking up on you in the West. As a kid in Iowa I could skate around on the river and fall through the ice and get pneumonia a couple of times and know that the holidays were near. Here, it was 98 degrees two weeks ago and I had ice in a bowl in front of the fan. The only way I sense a seasonal change is when the smog alerts taper off and my boys come home with their surfboards, looking a deeper shade of purple.

Even our arctic whales have trouble identifying the season. Consequently, they now mate year-round, any time of the day or night. (Which may account, in part, for our record attendance last summer.)

Still, I look forward to the Christmas crunch just as much as the next masochist. I don't even flinch at paying as much for the kids' gifts as my first car cost. (That was without the engine, which was always on the ground with a mechanic walking around it, mumbling strange words.)

I think the panic in my chest at Christmas actually stems from the realization that baseball try-outs can only be two months away. Then there go my evenings and Saturdays until July. This will be my 13th season as a manager. We move up to Colt League next, the 15- and 16-year-olds—*real* baseball!

Last season in Pony, we won the second half, but managed to boot the playoffs with some adroit managing. Gary listened to someone besides me and his numbers this year seem worthy of memorializing. (As a kid, I never made it past boys' baseball, because I couldn't spit through my teeth and touch myself spastically in 8 or 10 places at the plate.)

Anyway, my heir was runner-up for league pitching honors, led all in stolen bases and was the hero of the Memorial Weekend Invitational All-Star Tournament when, with us on the brink of defeat, he hit back-to-back homers to pull it out, then won the next game with a triple, two doubles and a single. Whew! I didn't come down off the top of the bleachers until Tuesday.

He still claims he wants to be a professional ball player. The next two years will tell. Who knows? A number of the boys who played in Craig's day are in major league ball now.

Craig is heavy into softball. He and his pals took second in a city league last year and are currently in first (I think that's first in beer-drinking for the year). Craig's partying has been curtailed. On his 21st birthday in March, everyone brought him bar beverages, but he was in bed with hepatitis. Picked it up on a camping trip to Mexico. He was one sick boy, let me tell you. He's still into heating and air conditioning work and claims that one day he will own us all.

Daughter Debbie emerged from five years in bank vaults and joined the glittering world of television last summer. She was on the sales staff of Channel 39, the NBC affiliate. She did her first commercial in September, appearing briefly and provocatively in a reclining chair, then had a short, but memorable fling with the new anchorman through the fall.

He took her to a dinner party for Dinah Shore and her picture wound up on the society page of the morning paper with Dinah and Ruth Buzzi. What smarts is that Lovae and I were there and we didn't get *our* picture taken. We didn't raise these kids to upstage us!

All this notoriety roused Deb's regular fella, Bill, and moved him to hurry to the jewelry store for a sparkler. I believe he was there before the place opened next morning after the paper came out. Mission accomplished. Debs quit the anchor *and* the TV station. She now devotes an unhealthy amount of time to her dogs (they look like timber wolves to me).

Sherrie, not to be outdone at 27, gave up cleaning her oven and growing plants and went to work for a friend who publishes a local business mag and helped him into bankruptcy. (That doesn't sound right, does it?) Anyway, she then took up modeling. Does noon fashions at a very "in" place in the valley for businessmen, known for its alluring waitresses. She loves it, and going under her married name of Doren, has accidentally been hustled by several of my good friends. But they're no match for the full-blooded Italians who buy the clothes off her back, then give them to her.

Her daughter—that would be *our* granddaughter—is four and cracks me up at least once a week. Angie's father Richard (just remarried) brought her to the door Halloween. I didn't know who she was at first. Then she whipped off her mask and said: "Hi, Gramps, can I come in?" After which she asked for a little something to drink (wonder where she gets that?). We gave her orange juice. She took a couple swallows and said, "Well, I've got to split now. Richard's out there in the cold waiting for me."

Lovae's horoscope, she announced, promises an early spring affair with a wealthy young lawyer. She is feeling quite confident and beguiling these days since having been propositioned in Bali by a professor of archaeology on her recent tour of the Far East.

No, I didn't sell the book. Lovae grew tired of waiting. So she and her cute little mother spent 23 days in November visiting Tokyo, Hong Kong, Singapore, Bangkok, and Bali, while the rest of us slept in unmade beds and ate out of the microwave. She picked up what appears to be a fairly permanent virus—and I came close to developing beriberi. We all are giving special thanks this holiday. The plane they were on to Singapore is the same one which went down five days later with all passengers lost.

Yes, I am still press agent for Shamu. For those of you who asked, or at least faked interest, I am corporate director of public relations for SeaWorld, Inc., a subsidiary of Harcourt, Brace, Jovanovich, Inc., a New York publishing company. In July, I received my five-year pin. No diamond in it. Business is good, in spite of our kicking the ticket price to $6.50, and we will top 2.2 million this year and approach 6 million for our three parks.

I kept stimulated by involvement with some TV shows originating from the park and meeting Dinah, and Anson Williams, and Valerie Perrine and Hal Linden (Barney Miller), and a reunion with a favorite star I met in my zoo days, the funny Arte Johnson, of *Laugh-In* fame.

I know you're behind in your shopping and wrapping and maybe even have wild eggnog parties to throw. So I'm going to cut this short for a change, hoping you'll appreciate my holiday thoughtfulness. Besides there's a full moon so I believe I'll take the little lady for a walk. Walking outdoors at night heightens the senses, and moonlight is a powerful aphrodisiac. (Well, we'll see!)

We wish you a fantastic holiday season once again and will be thinking of you.

Just remember as the New Year descends upon you what Ogden Nash once said: "Progress might have been all right once, but it has gone on too long."

Season's Greetings! 1978

Sorry to report that the inmates do not yet have the Christmas spirit around our asylum this year. What we seem to have are several cases of walking pneumonia, perhaps the pip and a suspected case of elm tree blight. The kids, not grandmother and me.

But we are descendants of a hardy stock. All are sure to recover by Christmas eve.

Craig is in a management training program with Cap'n Kidd's Fish 'n Chips, a local chain purchased last spring by SeaWorld to eliminate waste. Whatever the whales and sea lions reject, we fry up and sell in these fast-food outlets. (Just kidding!) This healthy-looking offspring of ours went into construction work with Sherrie's beau. Which was swell until the cement stopped coming. Craig claimed he couldn't make anything stick without cement. So now he's pursuing a new career. Frankly, I liked it better when he smelled like cement.

The 15-year-old, Gary, grew to 6 feet—one weekend recently. That was right after setting the California record for opening and closing the refrigerator in a single month. Darned if time didn't sneak up on us and the little guy graduated from junior high in

June. Maybe he simply signed an agreement not to come back in exchange for a "B" average. My brother had a similar arrangement in Iowa in the 1940s.

Now Gary's digging high school, discovering girls are softer than boys and concerned about living up to the reputation of the sisters, brother and cousins who preceded him. He's the eighth Seaton to stalk the halls at Point Loma High. Since he held the junior high track record for the 50, they recruited him heavily for football. But his knee's banged up, so he passed, and is strengthening it with weights for baseball. He figures Pete Rose makes more money than any football player.

Lord, what a baseball year we had (yes, here it comes, but only briefly as it's midnight out here in Shamu-land). I agreed to manage Gary's colt league squad while on a self-destruction kick as the year opened. We then managed to quickly lose our first 10 games. I was ready for the rubber room. I resigned. Wouldn't speak to my family. Wandered the streets aimlessly.

Then one full-moon night while sitting naked in the backyard, I told myself I was too old to give up. I've preached Hang In There and You'll Make It, Kid since I flunked chemistry in the 11th grade and had to buckle down to graduate. So I returned to the battleground and began kicking fannies. You guessed it, fans. We won the championship. (Give you chills?)

Let me tell you we play against some future pros. One of the kids from our league, Eddie Hook, was the first San Diego player taken in the major league draft this year...and the 37th player in the nation. His dad, one of our league's coaches, was just about the proudest father I have ever seen. For two weeks, he looked like he had a surgically-implanted grin.

Final baseball note: SeaWorld was the site of a night party on the eve of the major league All-Star game in July. We had dinner for 1600. During cocktails, a live television show originated from the park. In rounding up the players who were scheduled for interviews, I met Pete Rose, Greg Luzinski, Larry Bowa, Rod Carew, Jim Rice, Dave Winfield, and a few of the elite sluggers. Then had dinner with the owner of the White Sox and other millionaires. They kept saying: "This is the nicest place we've ever been! Where are the bugs?"

While I'm name-dropping, let's get it all out of my system. Big year for stars. In February, Lovae and I dined with Perry Como and crew during his Easter TV show from SeaWorld. Then in May, I had lunch with the Fonz, Henry Winkler. (We were mobbed when I took him on tour. Many young ladies clawed at me, probably mistaking me for John Travolta.)

Also did a show from the park with Anson Williams, and one day showed John Denver my whales. No one recognized Denver as we roamed the park until we attended the last Dolphin show. The mother sitting in the row in front of us turned and said: "Excuse me, but my daughter here says you're John Denver." He confessed he was. The lady shot back: "Well, you sure don't look like him!" Duh…

Several weeks ago, we took the baby walrus up to LA for *The Mike Douglas Show*. And tomorrow we're showing Eartha Kitt around. I suppose she'll sing me "Santa Baby…"

Not impressed? I don't blame you. Not one of them left a tip. Though the Fonz is second only to Travolta as the hottest TV star on the current scene, Perry was our favorite of the various celebs we've ever visited with at SeaWorld. He's in the all-time super-star crooner category and is truly Mr. Nice Guy.

I had to slip ice cubes down the back of Lovae's dress during cocktails after she posed with Perry for pictures. I hustled her onto other business when he asked if she had ever been fishing in Florida. She said she'd love to—and I know she's *allergic* to fish.

As a few of you may remember, my high school crush, Rose Marie Jun, was on the Como show for many years with the Ray Charles singers. Ray Charles himself was at dinner with us that evening, and we talked at length about her. He thinks she's the greatest. Said Rosie made a quarter of a million a year at one time. I took the same classes she did, so damned if I can figure out what went wrong.

I'm sure there are those who would criticize me for waiting 'til this late in the letter to mention the highlight of the year—our darlin' Debbie was married in June. She signed with Bill Ray, her suitor of the past several years, a young bank executive who's been trying to learn the combination to the vault.

The small church wedding was attended by 150 and should be paid for some time after the next presidential elections. We are slightly prejudiced, but she was the most beautiful bride since Liz Taylor rented her first white outfit. The reception was held at SeaWorld (surprise!) in a bayside pavilion under a full moon with a rock band which was kinda hard to see because my brother had sent about 20,000 flowers from his flower importing business in Miami. We had enough left over to enter a float in the Pasadena Rose Parade.

The smashing-looking couple honeymooned in Monterey, then purchased a country home in Lakeside about 30 miles outside of San Diego, furnished with the loot many of you nice people sent. Sister Sherrie was a radiant maid of honor and now has that look in *her* eye. We think that's great, but suggested she elope this time.

Neat footnote: Debs was married on our 30th anniversary, so I was allowed to drink twice as much that night. Lovae and I waited until two weeks ago to blow out an incredible 30 candles. We did it in New Orleans where I attended a public relations conference, then flew from Houston to Cozumel, the picturesque island in Yucatan. The blue-green water down there in Mayan country is among the world's best for diving. So after we dried off, we hopped over to Cancun, the Mexican Riviera it's called, but liked our unspoiled island better.

Would I consider my 50th birthday the low point of the year? Heck no. I enjoyed being here to help everyone celebrate it! The Mother Bear and I met my nephew Greg and pretty Patty in LA for a night on the town, which included a dynamite Liza Minnelli show at Universal Studios Amphitheater. Judy's kid was never one of my favorites, but she was the blue-ribbon most. She drew seven standing ovations. For the last, they dragged her out of the shower!

Then there were mini-weekends in Monterey and Lake Tahoe earlier in this action-packed year. Business trips were limited to three days in New York (coldest May day in NY in 25 years) and a quickie to Florida where I gashed my head open in the shower and bled all the way home. I stopped flying, I must tell you, after the PSA crash here. The town was in a real state of shock following that one! I saw the smoke while leaving SeaWorld that morning and thought it was another brush fire. For those of you who asked, it was not that close to us, since the crash occurred on the approach, and our casa is in the take-off pattern. One co-worker had canceled that flight to SD and was so shook, no one could get him out of church for three days!

Other joys of the year included quickie visits from the Stockstills (Lou was my writing mentor in DC.), now living in Florida; Ann Kacena, my oldest friend's sister I hadn't seen for 20 years; weekly visits from my granddaughter; and the "Immaculate Deception" in the first Charger/Raider game, which nearly gave me my first coronary!

The midnight candle burns low. I have a feeling some of you are drifting after three pages of shameless prose on how well life is going out here below the San Andreas fault. So I'll save the stories about shark-hunting for our new shark exhibit, and the record crowds my publicity drew to SeaWorld, for next time.

Lovae, our long-suffering den mother, and I wish you the merriest Christmas ever. Won't you think about visiting us in '79? If not, then how about a letter?

In the New Year, remember the old Muslim proverb: "Trust in Allah, but tie your camel."

Warmth, Cheers and Goodwill!

It's that time of year when, as inexorably as the red tide or the spread of Dutch elm disease, my annual letter makes its appearance across the land.

Lovae woke me up last weekend and announced it was December. I looked out the window and said: "Where's the snow? Where are the sleds and the snowmen of my childhood?" It was 80 degrees and climbing. She replied: "Get the lawn mowed and let's go shopping."

I went. But I think the playing of "Jingle Bells" during a smog attack should be outlawed.

Lovae, incidentally, discovered a new way of getting me up mornings. She opens the bedroom door and throws the cat on my bed. I sleep with the dog.

So, here we go with another of those three-page duplicated single-spaced rantings, crammed with news of the family triumphs of the past 12 months. (After listing the triumphs on separate sheets of paper in the last few moments, I believe two pages will do it.)

First, our neighbors, Bill and Laura Stevenson, say we're now officially Californians. We've learned to eat artichokes. Properly cooked, dipped in mayo, they are succulent! We're also hooked on avocados (world-class orchards abound 30 miles up the pike).

Bill likes to tell the story of how when they were first married, Laura drove the car to shop near Lake Murray one Saturday while he watched the ball game. When she came home, she announced: "There's water in the carburetor."

Bill rose and said: "Oh, c'mon, you don't know a carburetor from a spark plug. Where's the car?"

Laura said: "At the bottom of the lake."

October found us in Palm Springs, thanks to Master Charge, celebrating Lovae's 50th birthday at Marriott's pricey new Rancho Las Palmas. While old friends toasted her with margaritas, and a stoned mariachi band played the Tijuana version of "Happy Birthday," I smiled tearfully at my dark-eyed Libra mate and thought: "God, I hope I look that great when I'm 50!"

In June, Gary, our high school junior, shook us up badly by selling his surf board and getting a job. He worked as a ditch-digger and manure-spreader for a local landscape company before being laid off. "Guess I was in over my head," stated Gary.

He played third base in his first high school game last week and cracked a neat hit.

And that is the sum total of my baseball recap for the year. Colt League ended mercifully in June. I managed and coached for 14 years. Now I've hung up the spikes for good. When the Padres passed on me and selected Jerry Coleman to manage, it hurt a lot.

Besides, Charger-mania has overtaken us all. The stomping we gave Pittsburgh a few Sundays back was almost worth waiting 15 years for. I haven't first-hand witnessed such crowd hysteria since Iowa beat Notre Dame in 1939. I could get $300 easily for my ticket Monday night against Denver! I didn't think Fouts could bring us this far. If we win the AFC championship, I have to push a peanut to Pasadena with my nose.

Number one bachelor son, Craig, 23, either has something on the boss or is showing talent in the construction business. He wound up supervising the finish of his last building project. And he's scheduled for a stint after the first of the year in Sacramento. That's company HQ and the top man has promised to show him how to make a million. I hope there's something to it besides swamp land sales cuz I'm going to need help buying a 7,000-square-foot home with tennis courts, gym, and poolroom above the beach.

Daughter Debbie is happily married (isn't that boring?—but nice) and she and Billy spend spare hours fixing up their small acreage and scaring off rattlesnakes in Lakeside. They have attended several night classes, but still haven't found out what causes pregnancy. Having recently bought a red Mazda RX-7, they are tooting around everywhere before the bank comes for it.

Outgoing Sherrie (literally, she's always out going) plans to run off with her boyfriend, if she finds a rich one. She's back working at a bustling steak house patronized by fat salesmen and lean hoods, so she's not having much luck, though it's a slow night if she doesn't get two or three proposals (some even for marriage). She was interested in one good-looking, olive-skinned and charming gentleman until she saw the sign on his car parked out back: "Mafia Staff Car—Keepa You Hands Off!"

I promised myself I wouldn't get sickening about our granddaughter Angela. Just let me say she's not only the cutest six-year-old (blonde-hair, green eyes) south of LA, but she's smart. Don't discount her as the first woman president. At least from California.

She's an aspiring actress, as was her mother. (How many of you out there remember when Sherrie appeared in the Otto Preminger film *Tell Me That You Love Me, Junie Moon* with Fred Williamson? You had to be quick, but she was there.) Angela is scheduled to appear in "Dean Martin's Christmas in California" on NBC, December 13th. She was filmed in a SeaWorld skit in the play-area with Dean, Dom DeLuise, Ruth Buzzi, and Shirley Jones. If it winds up on the cutting room floor, I think I can count on getting fewer Christmas presents this year.

Bringing this show to San Diego was my *coup* of the year (maybe the only one). I spent about three months on it, including the sales pitching, fund-raising, site selection, pre-production planning and actual production. More details to moving a show out of Hollywood than you can shake a stick at, as we used to say in Ioway.

Recently, I did some publicity shots in the park with Andy Williams. Since we're both from Iowa, he asked to have a photo taken together. He's short. And could pass for a produce manager at Safeway. But like all Hawkeyes, a down-to-earth guy.

To top off the show biz portion of this self-indulgent saga, I appeared on *Hollywood Squares* in June and disgraced the family name by blowing the $8,000 Secret Square when I didn't know a line from Shakespeare (this will not come as a total shock to any of you who were my classmates).

It was worth the sweat and jangled nerves, though. I heard from my first girlfriend, in Iowa, my first boss at the *Cedar Rapids Gazette*, and a Navy chief I'd owed $10 to since 1947. The show even inspired boyhood pal, Butch Kacena to sell a few birds to pay for a lengthy call from his turkey ranch in Nebraska. (I think he wanted me to get him on the show, but he did worse than I did in 12th grade.)

I missed the eight grand by agreeing with Dick Van Patten— the dummy. I should have known better than to trust anyone with eight kids. I told the producers before I went on I hadn't been to college. I don't know what I'd have done with a sailboat and a trip to Canada anyway. I'm at the Padres games or Shamu show all summer.

But I gave it a whirl, shameless one that I am. However, I believe the stress of testing, auditioning, waiting under guard for

14 hours in the bowels of NBC, and going on before a live audience under glaring lights with eight stars and Big Bird staring at you while you prove to 20 million viewers that you're illiterate, is really more than a man of my station should subject himself to.

I did it only to amuse you, figuring you could use a few laughs (the Carter administration certainly hasn't provided us with as many as Nixon!) We *can* use the $700 Westinghouse microwave oven, though. Do you have any use for the pizza-making machine? Or the assorted vibrators? (Hmmm—maybe I should keep those.) I didn't miss *all* the questions.

My cousin Marilyn MacAllister called to say she thought I looked real cool on the show. I've always liked her. She's a teacher in Huntington Beach up the coast. I asked how she enjoyed her class this year. She said okay, but had one student so hopeless, she was tempted to write on his report: "This child should not be allowed to breed."

In a really fun deal, Lovae and I were invited on an inaugural flight by PanAm to New York. But not totally thrilled with spending much time in NY in July, we winged south on our own to spend a few days in DC with old friends and a stop at *Navy Times* to see survivors from the days when I was a fresh-faced Pentagon reporter. Then on to Orlando, Florida, to freeload with Neta and Lou Stockstill in their smashing new home, play a little clay-court tennis, and make another hop to the Virgin Islands for a few days of sailing, skin-diving and general-type vegetating at the St. Croix by the Sea.

We flew out of Puerto Rico into a hurricane, I should hasten to point out. I had planned to say a few things about the thrill of that death-defying ride in a 12-seater, but Lovae suggested that we not recount horror stories during the yuletide.

As many of you have asked, my dear mother is fine now that she's thrown away most of her pills and has a whisky now and then. Some days she recognizes me quite well.

That about covers it. (Seems my two-page letter was as unrealistic as my publishing a book in the 20th century!) Sure wish we could see more of you.

Have a jolly Christmas, hear?

And in the New Year take heed of the Chinese proverb: "To know the road ahead, ask those coming back."

Spread the Spirit of the Holidays!

We're joyous because it's December and miraculously, the Chargers are still in the race. The coming playoffs are the way pro football nuts know it's the holiday season. That and hearing Nat Cole singing about roasting his chestnuts at Sears since right after Halloween.

We got our pal Ronnie elected, and next thing, there I was this fall, back in front of the tube, where my wife says I qualified for the "Iron-man Couch Potato of the Year" award by watching 87 football games without fainting. But she exaggerates, as you know. Gets by with it because people say she's so cute.

The marriage is still intact—33 consecutive years now. I promised Lovae we'd go out a lot when the kids were grown. She says her back goes out more than we do. I did get her to renew for a year with a three-day trip to Mazatlan. We were guests of Pacific Southwest Airlines on their inaugural flight. The reason it was free, it turned out, was that we arrived on the first day of the rainy season.

Strictly VIP treatment, however. We were greeted by a brass band and whisked through customs. At our sparkling beach-front hotel, we were handed a pineapple full of booze, given a reception by the mayor and dinner (featuring roast boar on a spit), fireworks and a ceremony that included everything but a sacrificed virgin. (It turns out there are none left in Mazatlan.)

The kids try to keep us from stagnating, too, with a fun trip now and then. Like in March, they took us skiing at nearby Snow Summit, where I sprained every lateral ligament in my body and jarred loose two perfectly good fillings. I hadn't been on skis in 17 years. I fell six times the first day—three just putting my skis on.

When I awoke the next morning, everything hurt. And what didn't hurt, didn't work. But there had been a glorious 15-inch snowfall, and I eased into my frozen underwear and out to the slippery slopes, after a chorus of reassurances that everyone does better the second day. Craig and Billy (Deb's hubby, if you were not right up to date on the family tree) have been to Snow Summit numerous times. They later said they were pretty sure I was the only person ever to come down from the number 4 lift all the way on my back. And Gary added helpfully, "Certainly the only *grandfather!*"

Lovae being the smarter half, as you always suspected, stayed smugly in our warm condo, cooking chili for the ravenous crew and keeping happy (we suspect) with a nip of the sherry.

We do try to stay active in the battle against aging. But often I feel like the morning after…and I haven't been anywhere. I'm kidding, of course. I'll never grow old, as those of you who remember my youthful appearance will be quick to agree. I'm a little concerned though: A fortune teller offered to read my face the other day.

Actually, I won my first tennis trophy last spring. The children, who only see me after I've had a few Jack Daniels and snore on the couch, think I bought it. I was only a runner-up in the B Division, so suppose I shouldn't have had it mounted on the hood of our new Olds.

Then I seriously damaged my health-nut image by coming down with a flare up (and it's not easy to come *down* with a flare *up!*) of osteomylitis in October. First time that ole devil in my leg got me in 14 years. I was caught hobbling around on crutches by my pal since 8th grade, Butch Kacena, the Nebraska flash, who dropped in here, after seven years, wearing hand-tooled cowboy boots and escorting a gorgeous blonde he tried to pass off as his wife. Hocked half-a-truck-load of turkeys to pay for the trip out here and go stomp-jumping in Tijuana one last time. He pretended to be sympathetic to my handicap, but left for the border after dinner in spite of my offer to show him our old California missions.

SeaWorld, still my place of employment, had a record year, topping $100 million in revenues for the first time. As a result of voting for the peanut farmer, we wound up netting about a dollar three-ninety-eight. Though we had a good year, I had to reduce my PR staff. My bosses' philosophy is that two insecure employees will do the work of four.

Had a few celebrities in the park as I look back (go get a beer if you can't face name-dropping time). Little Nellie from *Little House on the Prairie* came in and stripped down to take a bikini shot with the dolphins for some reason. She had the whitest skin I *ever* laid orbs on. Looked like she'd just been dug up. One of the trainers said: "You'd think anybody spent that much time on the prairie would have gotten *some* sun."

Shari Lewis, Lamb Chop's mother, dropped in to swim with the dolphins, pleading she was out of material for her syndicated column. In gratitude, she invited me to bring my wife to a free dinner at her Beverly Hills mansion. Cost me $500 for a new dress, pearls to set it off, plane tickets and a shoe shine. Upon arrival, we inspected her pre-Colombian art and, after cocktails, were ushered to a dining room table looking like it was set for the Queen mum. The meal for her six guests was sumptuous. (Said son-in-law later: "I trust they didn't serve *lamb chops!*")

Other tough duty included spending several days talking Cathy Lee Crosby into riding Shamu for the popular TV show *Those Amazing Animals*.

In February we'll be taping the *SeaWorld Animals Awards Show* from here with a few celebs like Loretta Swit, Ed Asner, Betty White, and your favorite dog "Boomer."

Our kids are doing fine. Nothing about them to interest the *National Enquirer* this year. Fortunately for Debbie and Bill, they have some chickens to fall back on if real estate refinancing continues to dry up. It would be a shame to eat my favorite: a rooster named Colonel Sanders.

Sherrie and her daughter Angela have taken a fancy new condo as their abode for the Eighties. Sher's apparently making more in tips than the government suspects.

Big Craig ended his quest for a 30-hour week by going into cable television. He's selling for Mission Cable, world's largest, and not doing that bad. Also, his gang won the city three-pitch championship again this year. But somehow, in spite of his softball trophy and father's cleft chin, he has managed to remain a laid-back bachelor.

So has Gary. But he only graduates from high school in June. He doesn't date much—probably because of his hearing handicap—from playing his stereo and sitting in the first 10 rows at the rock concerts. I asked him what he learned the past four years while I was in the salt mines. He said: "I've learned something very important. If you want to be the life of the party, associate yourself with very dull people." He hates his government teacher. Sez you could walk through the waters of his mind without getting your feet wet.

And Lovae, well, she stays cool through the whole hysterical scene by making like a duck—unruffled on the surface and paddling like hell underneath.

The Seaton tribe wishes you the Happiest Holidays ever—and heavily suggests you stock up on dehydrated foods in case the ex-cinema cowboy can't stop this out-of-control sleigh ride!

A thought for the New Year from Emerson: "Always do what you're afraid to do."

Greetings...

It's me—the star-struck Hawkeye who migrated westward 21 years ago and landed about 125 miles short of Hollywood. But who's now a close friend of Dean Martin's. I trust you saw our TV special last week. The one featuring Dean-o (he told me to call him that) and all our fish. Because if you didn't, I haven't got anything to top it this year, so you may want to grab a jolt of caffeine to help you through the next three pages written in the first person.

To get on with it, I shook myself out of a summer lethargy and put together a deal that resulted in an NBC show titled: *Dean Martin's Christmas at SeaWorld*. If that sounds like I'm well connected in show biz, forget it. I was sitting on the curb outside the main gate, waiting for someone to take me to lunch, when this gold Caddy pulled up, and an Italian-type rolled down the window and asked if I'd be interested in buying a television special for a few *lira*.

The few *lira* translated into 100,000 American bucks. When I told my boss, he snorted: "That's a lotta clams. It better be great." I laughed (you have to laugh at those kind of comments around here) and didn't sleep all night for weeks.

Since our sea lions, Clyde and Seamore, along with Shamu, were featured more than Dean, the show turned out to be more like a 60-minute commercial for our sun-splashed park. Now the boss is laughing again. And I sleep a lot.

For those of you who watched A *Charlie Brown Christmas* instead of our show, you didn't miss a *great* production. But NBC told us it was the highest-rated show they'd had in a long time. Attracted between 35 and 40 million viewers. That's not chopped chicken liver, fans. We'd have doubled that if we had used a car-chase scene through the park and an octopus groping a sea maid. Anyway, the boss insinuated my job is secure to the end of the year. We have a Rose Bowl Game bet at that time. Guess who took Iowa? I'll never learn....

The boss has been a little touchy since passing age 45 this year. Complains his love life has gone from: tri-weekly...to try weekly...to try weakly.

Thank God, my probationary period is about over at SeaWorld. I'm due a 10-year pin in 1982. I'm looking forward to wearing my new seal-skin sports coat and alligator shoes to the ceremony.

I selected a whole new wardrobe on my own this fall after the boss gave me a book called *Dress for Success*. (My Nehru jackets and cardigans *were* beginning to look tacky.) Found some great buys at a discount clothing store. Lovae admitted she liked the three-piece charcoal suit—a $225 number on sale for half-price (with alterations, taxes, and an annuity for the salesman, I picked it up for $235). She said it made me look conservative and responsible and like someone who never uses incense, but always uses "interface, dichotomy and low profile." The corduroy sport coat, contrasting corduroy pants, negative heel shoes, patterned shirt open at the collar, however, she felt would lead people to believe I was a salesman of rubber sex aids.

Speaking of Lovae, it's good to have her home for Christmas. She left the first of November. Said she was going to the Far East for a month. I asked her if it was because I let the lawn turn brown. (We haven't communicated much since that happened during an exceptionally warm summer, in which I spent most leisure hours between the tennis courts and the pool.)

She said it was no *one* thing, but included a growing sense of futility, chronic exhaustion, loss of control, boredom, frustration, loss of motivation, anger, depression, lack of feeling, inability to made decisions, and the fact that I had failed to set out the trash cans again on Tuesday. I offered to take her to Old Town to a new Mexican restaurant, but she left that evening.

Lovae, her mother and sister from Oklahoma had a dream trip, in all seriousness. They started in Tahiti and left money throughout Australia, New Zealand, Hong Kong, Bangkok, Bali, Singapore, and Tokyo, stopping on the return in the Hawaiian Islands (I suppose to heist a savings and loan).

By the first of December, the boys and I suffered what the doctor described as "prolonged negative stress" and a combined weight loss of 24½ pounds. But while she was over there clicking her chopsticks, I fondled my electric blanket and looked at the positive side: I learned 11 ways to prepare tuna, plant care, sock sorting, how to extinguish a bacon grease fire, basic Spanish (the Mexican cleaning lady and I spent a lot of time in hand gestures), and why you never shop at the super market when you're hungry. Incidentally, I spent $80 the first time I dashed through FedMart prior to Monday night football and could put everything I bought in the glove compartment.

Four weeks. That's the longest we ever survived without her. And we did darned well, she admitted on her return, after conducting a white-glove inspection at 11:00 P.M.

I've since raised her allowance $10 a week and offered to bring in the SeaWorld horticulturist for a little yard rejuvenation. I sure don't want her going through any of that middle-age crazy stuff again.

Some of you who haven't seen my kids for 5 or 10, or even 20 years would be amazed—if only at how much they don't look like me.

Gary, the 18-year-old, is into Zen and eating elm bark. He likes all things cosmic. And tropical fish. If he plugs into my electrical circuit with another of his 100-gallon tanks, I'm going to have to find a night job. He has always had an affinity for wildlife and is concerned over the threat to our endangered species. For Christmas his brother's getting him a tie depicting the last carrier pigeon being shot.

This summer, Gary established a new family record for shortest time in one job: two and one-quarter hours. Washing dishes at the pizza parlor. That broke a personal 35-year-old record I held since 1945: six hours cutting the kidneys out of freshly slaughtered hogs at the Wilson Packing Plant in Cedar Rapids, Iowa. I quit after lunch.

Gary eagerly signed up for junior college the very next day. Then, withdrawing his savings of $175, he drove to the mountains to spend a week getting back to nature, away from the crass commercial world. Half way up during a rainstorm, his Buick spun off the road and stuck in the roadside mud. No one would help him, so he called the tow truck. The driver charged him $150. Gary was home by the next day, mumbling something about going into a monastery.

Craig, at 25, abandoned his crowd's philosophy that any man who has to work is a failure. He signed on as a driver-salesman for Coca-Cola and has the back strain to prove it. Tough work at 5:30 A.M., but he's been promised a promotion the first of the year.

He still, apparently, is the fastest cat in Ocean Beach. No chick has caught him, anyway. He's been giving a lot of thought to life these days. Said it's kind of sad to know there are 24 hours in a day, and only one is the *Happy Hour*. What's really depressing, though, is the kid took five tennis lessons this fall and beat me last week in a set of singles. I've only been playing 39 years and thought I was beginning to improve. I play three times a week and am ranked 1,429 on the computer, well ahead of all but a few famous pros who are in full-care homes.

My ageless daughters have been accused of slipping across the border for glandular shots. Actually, they just have beautiful genes. And follow my vitamin program with a missionary's zeal. Both live a quarter of a tank away, but check in regularly, if only to see whether I've upgraded my taste in wine, or gotten them signed by Universal Studios. (I've never told them I only know the director of *tour buses* there.)

Sherrie will soon qualify for retirement at the restaurant where she innocently zaps lustful men out of $50 and $100 tips with her dazzling smile and long legs. As a waitress, that is. Neat place—one of our *in* steak houses. I hated to have to stop hanging out there. She attracts dudes from both coasts, it seems. Her latest interest is flying back from Virginia for a serious visit New Year's Day. Her psychic says this is "the One."

My granddaughter, Angela, is eight, an "A" student, and a terrific skater. Won her first trophy in competition last month! (Don't you hate when this bragging comes?) Anyway, I'm taking no chances and am saving money to attend the Winter Olympics in '88.

Debbie re-entered the work force this year. Went to work for this doctor who turned out to be slightly demented. And had a daughter just like him for an assistant. Deb escaped to a calmer, normally insane position with my financial planner. (I called her boss and asked: "What should we plan this year?" She said: "To make more money, so we can plan something.") I'm not greedy. All I want is as much money as my kids think I have.

Okay, folks, the end is in sight. (Don't take my word for it. Go to any beach and see the pollution.)

Several quick bits of good news: My mother will celebrate her 80th birthday in February. Says she can remember when she danced with Ronnie Reagan on a double date in the 1930s. She doesn't look even 65, really. That's what having no bad habits will do, she keeps reminding me. We think she chews a little when she's alone, though. She was born on a farm in Iowa. To this day, she still puts on her coat to go to the bathroom.

One of Mom's next-door neighbors at the retirement home is quite senile. I passed her open door and saw her sitting there, smiling the other day. "Hi, Mable," I said. "How are you this afternoon?" She blinked at me and finally gave a little smile. I stepped in and asked, "Do you know who I am?"

She smiled sweetly and said, "No, but if you'll go to the front desk they'll tell you."

Brother Mark's outstanding daughter, Linda caught a man during a Sadie Hawkins Day dance in Anaheim. They will be married here Saturday. She's a teacher in the LA area and still movie-star pretty. Her husband-to-be, Lynn, passed inspection by all 21 of the Seaton clan, and is warmly welcomed. Some say he has money. I don't know how much, but when he broke his leg playing tennis, he took a cab to the hospital—and told the driver to wait.

My brother arrived last night from Miami. Had a little delay getting the money tree through security. His wholesale flower business is doing well. On a recent return from a successful business trip in Canada hawking carnations from Bogota he had so much money stuffed in his suitcase, customs mistook him for an athletic free agent.

My only trip this year was to a March television convention in New York City (we drew straws at the office to see who had to get the long underwear out of mothballs this time). While visiting briefly at the Hilton with Mike Douglas—he's done several shows at all three SeaWorlds—a fantastic face appeared next to his. Mike sez to me, "Oh, Bill, do you know this young lady?" I gasped, "Brooke Shields!" When she learned who I was with, she gushed that she just *loved* Shamu and threw a whale of a hug on me. Three NY television cameramen fired away probably thinking I was *someone*.

I walked three blocks in the snow afterward before I realized I'd left my overcoat.

The next evening, several of us attended the Mickey Rooney hit *Sugar Babies* with President and Mrs. Reagan. I don't think the Reagans knew they were with us. I barely saw the play over the Secret Service men.

So it goes in the world of flackery. But listen, if you don't think PR works, look at all the people who travel to Florida in the summer.

In closing, I must tell you my bright new secretary won $10,000 on *Battle Stars* last week. This so inspired me, I'm going on the show early in 1982. Stay glued to your sets—it may be your last chance to see me make a fool of myself on network TV.

Hope you and your whole bunch have the most fantastic holidays ever. And remember: "Too many people go through life running from something that isn't after them."

Joyous Yuletide Greetings!

Jogging home from the beach Sunday, I was reminded that Christ's birth observance is almost here. A speeding Porsche that narrowly missed me bore a bumper sticker reading: "I Brake for Reindeer." The *bird* the dazzling blonde driver flipped me in no way resembled a Partridge in a Pear Tree.

I keep waiting for it to snow. Which is not likely, I suppose, at 75 degrees. But even a light frost would help an old Midwesterner get in a Christmas mood. Our son, Gary, is in the kitchen, sorting through exotic punch recipes and singing: "Hark the herald angels sing—doo-dah...doo-dah!" But that doesn't quite cut it.

I did venture out to do some Christmas shopping one night. I bought a football video game, a hockey video game, and a Pac-man video game. I also got something for the kids.

Then Lovae sent me to the post office with my bonus money to buy stamps for these letters. I couldn't believe the *slow* service. The guy in line ahead of me turned around and asked if Iran had released the hostages yet. Twenty cents a stamp and they still manage to run in the red. It just doesn't make sense—like Howard Cosell singing "Silent Night."

I don't mean to complain. We have so much to be thankful for this year. Our kids turned out real well when you consider those you see around you. A friend got a report from school that said: "Your child sets low personal standards, then consistently fails to achieve them."

Like many, we're going a little light on the Christmas gifts this season. It's been one of those frustrating years financially. There's always the usual minor disasters. The dishwasher gave up the ghost, our carpeting disintegrated before our very eyes, and the day Lovae's Cougar quit running Gary's Buick died, as if in a sympathetic pact.

Lovae has maintained a sense of humor through it all, though. For my birthday she gave me a new book entitled: *101 Things You Can Do During Station Breaks*.

Sister-in-law, Marcie, was over the other night helping me get rid of some aging vodka and asking if we knew whether debtors' prisons were still cold and rat-infested. She had just received her gas and electric bill. She claims the difference between the 1930s and the 1980s is that it takes more money to be poor now.

As you may recall, my brother Mark operates a fairly legitimate wholesale flower business out of Miami. I visited him earlier in the year, and he nearly destroyed my liver. Told me over an Alka-Seltzer how the Feds keep searching his flower boxes shipped in from South America, certain that he's smuggling drugs. But he's clean. Doesn't even use pot, though he was robbed twice this year and is stressed. Says cocaine is God's way of telling you you've got too much money.

SeaWorld felt the impact of the recession—annual attendance is down about five percent. We're doing better than most of the nation's tourist attractions, however. The boss didn't go overboard on Christmas gifts this year, though: Gave me a bar of soap on a rope.

Daughter Debbie surprised herself and advanced from secretary to insurance adjuster last summer and is mad about her work. Her boss is mad about *her*. He's been lifting weights trying to get as buffed as her husband, Billy.

Deb had a little surgery at Scripps Hospital last month. She's laid up for a few weeks, but is mending well on my vitamin program. She's busy raising puppies and mice on their acreage, which Billy developed a hernia fixing up so impressively. My son-in-law can do just about anything. He told me, after quaffing a bottle of Gallos Rhine, he always lived by the belief that nothing is impossible. I asked him if he'd ever tried dribbling a football.

Deb is an accomplished artist, so we hope she'll be able to go cold turkey on her "soaps" and get back to water colors now. (Said she never realized there were over 10 million unemployed until she looked at the ratings for *General Hospital*.)

Sherrie hobnobbed with the Reagan entourage at the Santa Barbara ranch several weekends this year. She's long-time friends with the radio-TV guy at the White House. She got the royal treatment. She said the inside feeling is that Reagan needs to look for a new astrologer.

Jupiter, planet of good fortune, has not been doing much for her otherwise. Her VW breaks down twice a month, the IRS is seeking a cut of her tips and only 8 or 10 people are eating out a night now. Her "ex," an inspiration to all those who call in sick, walk slow and change jobs seasonally, does not lend much support. But she isn't discouraged, she told me in a rambling two-hour conversation recently. Agrees with Woody Allen that 80 percent of life is showing up.

This will be the first year her daughter Angela doesn't believe in Santa. Actually she got suspicious last year on Christmas eve when we called the North Pole and got a recorded message saying, "Hi, this is Santa. I'm not in right now but—" She's a darling kid, still winning ribbons for skating. And shows flashes of scholastic originality. Her teacher in health class asked what she did to protect her teeth. "I watch out for kids pushing at the drinking fountain," she said.

Gary just moved into a fancy apartment that costs about the same as it would to put him through medical school. He's working in the tennis pro shop at Vacation Village, which is great for meeting girls, but doesn't contribute much toward social security, so pop helps out. You might say I have almost a Siamese-twin relationship with my son. We're joined at the wallet.

I asked him what his guiding philosophy is now that he's looking at the last 30 days of his teens. He offered this: "You don't burn up your blanket to get rid of fleas."

Craig's back in construction work, relieved that the depression is nearing an end. He's into tennis and health food, too. He's not a confirmed bachelor, but he agrees with W.C. Fields who said: "Women are like elephants. They're nice to look at but who wants to own one?"

My business trip to Florida is always a kick. After PR meetings with the staff in Orlando, George and Sandy Becker procured a fabulous new condo for me next door to Pam Shriver. The Beckers and I ate hot dogs and guzzled a beer and sat at court-side to see the women tennis pros play for mega bucks. Martina won and scowled a lot. I missed much of the court action. Man-woman Renee Richards, sat next to me.

And then there was the annual spring trip to the Hindes casa in Borrego desert, which is always worth some laughs with the other survivors of the Africa trek in 1970, during which we made Kodak rich.

I took my bride to a football banquet for our 34th anniversary. She wasn't too thrilled, even though we had a nice chat with Kellen Winslow. I have since lunched several times with him and an editor friend to discuss doing a book on His Greatness.

Lovae got back at me. On my birthday she left to run some errands and announced that my gift would be delivered shortly. A guy from Sears showed up before noon with a new washing machine.

Didn't have much truck with other celebrities this year. My favorite, of course, is our own Joan Embery. Been working with her and a NY producer on a new cable TV series called *Animal Express*.

In May, I showed Dolores Hope around the grounds. During her whale kiss, Shamu missed her cheek and banged his nose into her ear, hurting her slightly. If she weren't so rich, she might have sued. A lovely lady, Mrs. Hope was telling me of her husband's great energy as he nears 80, and the fact that he's always on the road. Said she told him if he didn't stay home more, she was going to sell the damned house (that circular multi-million dollar eye-catcher on the mountaintop in Palm Springs).

I was shocked to receive a Christmas card from the Hope family. Really cool!

Luck was with us regarding the new *Simon and Simon* television show CBS taped here in August, in which the bad guys swiped one of our dolphins. It aired the week after they were rated the number one show in the nation. Got a lot of SeaWorld plugs in for a network show. After Jeannie Wilson held my hand, I had to go get a double B-12 shot.

We're currently plotting a major national publicity campaign for the opening of our most costly addition ever—"The Penguin Encounter"—a $7 million fantasy of our bird people. Might have Walter Cronkite here for the opening Memorial weekend.

After that, I hope to grab a vacation and slip into DC to see if I'm still loved and remembered. Also to check on a guy we admire much, our former mayor, Senator Pete Wilson.

I went in to complain to the boss last week that we never seem to get caught up on our PR tasks, though I've assembled the best staff in the West. He handed me a card that read: "If it was easy, you wouldn't be making all this money."

I was a young man when I started this letter. Now, before the ghost of Christmas past appears, I must be off to the post office.

My family wishes yours the best old Santa ever! Remember in the New Year: "Love is grand. Divorce is a hundred grand."

Oh, Holy Night...

1983

The once "futuristic" year 1984 looms...

And I'm still not famous.

But then a lot of weird predictions have failed to materialize. (Think how George Orwell must feel!)

Forty years ago, guys with big hair and horn-rimmed glasses with pencil protectors in their shirt pockets were running around saying: "By 1984, we'll see bus service between LA and Mars. Portable phones will be the rage. Receptionists in New York City will be civil. And millions will have a computing machine in the home."

One out of four isn't bad. (In a moment of mental confusion, I bought an Eagle II home computer that will be paid off sometime after the turn of the century.)

On the other hand, 40 years ago, who'd have predicted I'd be having dinner with Brooke Shields? Certainly not Ms. Shields. (But more on that later—I don't want to start with the heavy name stuff and risk losing you so early.)

Otherwise, as my tennis partner, Colonel Jim, always says: Health's fine. Morale's high. And the yacht hasn't been repossessed yet.

I turned 55 without a lot of fuss or hysteria. Much hilarity at the office party when the candles set off the sprinkler system. As my 25-year-old secretary so helpfully pointed out, "You qualify for free flu shots this year, sir."

All the kids in the park call me "sir" now out of respect for great age—as if I were some historical figure.

Same jazz at home. The other night, I slipped into a rented tux before giving out a "best supporting actress" award at the Starlight Musicals banquet. I asked Lovae if she didn't think I looked rather distinguished with my silver hair and red cummerbund. She said I was beginning to like more like my passport photo. Perhaps my vaccination against middle-age is wearing off.

June marked another milestone in our marriage. Lovae's been frying my eggs for 35 hilarious years now. She also has become a regular contributor to Ann Landers.

We celebrated our anniversary in the colorful, bay-side Presidential Suite at nearby Vacation Village. Tried to recapture the magic of our wedding night. *This* time I went in the bathroom and cried.

Instead of a trip to Tahiti, I bought Lovae a new backyard. I had let things go while working on Chapter Two of my epic. Our victory garden was beginning to look like a stretch of the Gobi Desert.

Now she spends countless sunny hours in our new dichondra, murdering snails big enough to saddle and ride. Her vegetables thrive. Like any proud gardener, she comes up with some strange concoctions. Yesterday, after the Chargers loss, she bandaged my wrists and made us zucchini daiquiris.

Being a Chargers fan, I found, builds strong character. It teaches a person that if you try hard enough and long enough, you'll still lose.

Know what else is depressing? Living with someone who never ages, when you're the one who spends a hundred a month on vitamins and Jojobe oil. All of Lovae's little atoms and chromosomes seem so happy together. She has not changed perceptibly since I attended her high school graduation in Virginia in my sailor suit with a pint of Four Roses and seaman first class George Moxley.

Her habits haven't changed a lot either. She still has a thing about neatness. She actually irons my jockey shorts.

She's enjoying a quiet house these days. This is her first year without boarders. We're down to a pregnant alley cat (who is using up most of my retirement money on Meow Mix she shares with a bullying band of overweight pigeons). Gary evacuated his teens in January. For his birthday, we gave him a matched set of luggage. And a bus ticket.

Truthfully, though, we miss him. Not his music. But him. The doctor says adult hearing sometimes takes up to a year to return to normal, so I haven't given up hope. He stopped by Thanksgiving. Ate like he'd just walked from Yuma, Arizona.

Gary's tall, lean, and well-buffed. For fun, we began comparing biceps. I asked him if he didn't think I could still be a male model. He said: "Sure, Dad. For *Smithsonian* magazine."

I won't comment on his work habits. Let's just say he's a rest-aholic. He watches sunsets from his pad in Ocean Beach, just beyond the horizon zone, and writes poetry to a charming French girl who admires his wavy hair and innovative nature. She finds him something of a contradiction, though. Says he opens a six-pack to watch Masterpiece Theater.

Number one son, Craig, made the choice between being a man or a spouse this year. He's decided to permanently share his electric blanket with a dazzling blonde lady of Nordic extraction who laughs at his jokes and lets him win at tennis. This being a first, he's taking no chances. She fell for his line about a lifetime

SeaWorld pass, and they'll be getting hitched next year. They make a striking couple, if I do say so. We're happy he's giving up his surfboard for Miss Dana.

Craig's with Pacific Scene: big, filthy rich, residential builders. The houses he built last year are still standing, so the boss made him assistant superintendent.

We occasionally bang the ball around together, keeping me in shape so I'm not embarrassed to enter an occasional hacker's tennis tournament. I waltzed off with a decent Kodak camera as runner-up in the summer SeaWorld tourney. Was soundly thrashed in the final by an 18-year-old fish pond cleaner.

Like my boss, Mr. Schultz, says: "No matter how good you get, there's always someone out there who can whip your butt." An ex-jock, Schultz is tough-minded in running a large, productive marketing staff. He knows the price of success, though—ulcers, high blood pressure, hyper-tension, nervous tics. Our staff has them all. He seems surprised I'm still working there. Tells people that when I started, the company car was a Schwinn.

This was the Year of the Penguin for us, as you must have heard, unless you've been on embassy duty in Vladivostok. After much crotch-scratching and ceiling-gazing, we finally built an Antarctic replica, housing 300 of the little fellas in dinner jackets. Blew a cool $7 million. We opened with a week of parties, figuring what the hell, if the exhibit didn't draw, it would be our last decent meal anyway. Reaped a ton of publicity. Been featured in TV specials, Merv's show, *Good Morning America,* the *Today* show, *CBS Evening News, People* magazine, etc.

For the black-tie fund-raiser opening night, I talked Brooke Shields into attending (through our contact, Joan Embery). Hired me a big limo, and Lovae and I picked Brooke and her mother up at their temporary rental in La Jolla. *Entertainment Tonight* covered our arrival and tour of the penguins. We shared Brooke with the Charger's Rolf Benirschke during dinner. All the SeaWorld officers at the next table tried to be cool. Kept dropping their food, sneaking peeks at the young beauty.

Brooke is gorgeous to the max. And tall. I stood on tippy-toes to kiss her cheek "goodnight." She's a lovely, fun, unspoiled beauty, folks. Replaced Perry Como at the top of our "favorite stars" list.

Mother Teri let us auction a kiss from Brooke. One drunk bid $1,100, so we tried another. It went for $1,500 and the guy's wife threatened to leave him.

We had a lot of glitter at Shamu-land this year. Just finished working with Cathy Rigby as part of her coming TV special. Frank Robinson, manager of the Giants, was one of the guests. I gave him a few tips on how I won the Colt League championship in '79. He didn't smile.

In September we entertained Phyllis Diller, Pam Bellwood (*Dynasty* show), and Ann Jillian (*Jennifer Slept Here*). They were taping a few daring acts for "Circus of the Stars," which you'll see on your tube this month. Phyllis was a kick, as you might suspect. She arrived looking like she had her hair arranged in a lobotomy clinic. During lunch, she gave me her book *The Joys of Aging— and How to Avoid Them*.

I showed Maude Adams around one summer Saturday (*Octopussy* with James Bond). She's into tennis. I told her of my always ready willingness to rip off a few sets. She said she'd be in touch. She was—sent me a case of tennis balls and a note asking if I'd mind escorting her mother around when she arrived from Sweden.

Jimmy Stewart and his wife were other summer visitors. He wasn't too loquacious. While he and I rested on a nearby bench, I told him how much I enjoyed his westerns and the Hitchcock thrillers. I asked if he really enjoyed making them. He said, "Yup." Long pause. Did he want to pet a penguin? "Nope."

Last spring, we were stunned to be invited aboard the Royal Yacht Britannia for a bit of ale and a peek below deck. Some canoe. The *motor launch* was fancier than anything I'd ever sailed. Looked for the Queen. She and Phil were in Tijuana, or somewhere.

In October, while Lovae and her sweet little mother were in Oklahoma, staring at the hole on their land where the oil's supposed to come up, I bopped out to a Neil Diamond concert. Old Navy friend Marshall Gelfand is the singer's business manager. He seated me in the 12th row, where I wouldn't miss the effects of the opening and closing cannon blasts. Awesome performance, I must say. I wore my black jeans and shoes with the turquoise buckles and seemed to fit right in.

Speaking of big names (as I still seem to be), daughter Sherrie was catatonic for three days over missing Clint Eastwood at her restaurant on her night off. Probably best she did though. She deflated the egos of both Vince Edwards and Mohammad Ali by serving them and not recognizing who they were!

She still runs a personal limo service to the skating rink and is building a trophy case weekends for my talented granddaughter. Cover-girl attractive as Sher is, she says it's been such a lousy year she wouldn't be afraid to let anyone read her diary. Gave up her long-distance love affair in Virginia. Is having the phone surgically removed from her ear.

Daughter Deb was voted the best-looking insurance claims adjuster in town—by her boss. He has such a crush on her, he has to go to the bar every afternoon to ease the ache. (His doctor told him he should stop drinking—but he claims there are more old drunkards than old doctors.) Deb only drinks at the Fountain of Youth. That's a bar in Santee. Says her goal is to die young—at an old age.

She enjoys country living on the once weed-choked acreage they have fixed up in Lakeside. Balks at the Rattlesnake Roundup though. Her husband tries to get her to play more tennis to keep that hour-glass figure. She thinks washing, scrubbing, ironing, and weeding will do it.

Son-in-law Billy became one-third owner of his mortgage loan company, so is on his way to fame and fortune. Refers to it as going from the screw-ee to the screw-er. He's earned the promotion. Finances were so lean last spring, he and Deb gave up drinking. We stopped by one Saturday and caught them trying to wring out a piece of fruit cake.

I sympathize. Last New Year's, I resolved to give up smoking, drinking and sex to work on my book. It was the most terrifying two hours of my life!

Have the Happiest Holiday ever. And in the New Year ahead, remember: "If everything's coming your way, you're in the wrong lane."

Noel!
Noel!

1984

I'm sitting here enjoying a few quiet hours with my money before it departs.

Early in the year, I called my children together and told them they should plan to work for a long time, as it didn't look like I was going to be rich. Sherrie said: "That's all right, Dad. Money isn't everything."

Craig retorted: "It isn't?"

Sher shot back: "Heck no. Health counts 2 percent."

For Father's Day, the kids addressed my card: To Whom It May Concern.

And now it's national indigestion season, according to the bicarbonate industry. I hate to sound like old Scrooge, but hearing the first yuletide commercial the day after Thanksgiving this year was about as welcome as a new kidney stone.

One needs some time to go through the decompression chamber. We just hauled away the bottles from the World Series celebration. (Lovae's afraid if we win the pennant again, I'll develop a drinking problem...claims my bar bill in October was longer than my phone bill.)

I had fervent hopes of regaining my health and sprinting a 10-minute mile again. Now the eggnog and rum's flowing, and it's time for my end-of-the-year Niagara of words (and Sahara of thought?).

I'm sure not the party guy I used to be. I usually nod off about 10 o'clock, overworked as I am on the job (had the bends twice this year). Lovae loves to talk and dance into the wee hours. New Year's Eve she says she's fixing my martinis with a twist of No-Doz.

I guarantee you I stayed awake the night we won our first World Series game. I was stuck in the traffic and rioting 'til midnight. We had to put up our youngest as security for game tickets.

Couldn't get SeaWorld plugged on national TV during the Series. I should have rented PR friend Dave Nuffer. He was all over the tube, waving 20-foot signs that blocked out two rows of spectators before they finally took him away. He's certifiable at home games. Believe me, anyone who went through the playoffs and World Series with our team this season, can now face a firing squad without a blindfold or a cigarette.

It was a dizzying plunge from the Padres penthouse to the Chargers basement. Last spring, in anticipation of them finally making it to the Super Bowl, I bought three Chargers season tickets (at about the same price as the down payment on a Maserati). After the Denver debacle I was ready for a straitjacket. When Kellen Winslow went down against the hated Raiders, then Fouts fell, I wanted to open a vein.

Opponents hold our defense in about the same esteem cheetahs hold gazelles with limps. Quick snacks, no sweat. I'm outta there, Chargers…history.

But a jolly thing did happen to us this year. In June, number one son, Craig, and darlin' Dana reproduced a neat little male-type Gemini human who comes over and burps on me several times a week. Nolan William. Look for him soon on Gerber's jars. Maybe 1986 SeaWorld commercials. I'm slightly demented about this kid.

Son Gary turned 21 and continues his search for a higher meaning in life. I don't quite know how he's going to find it, squeezing soda cans and watching *Gilligan's Island* reruns, but who am I to intrude on the mystic ways of the young? He's easing into the job market by spending a few days a week in sales at the Vacation Village Pro Shop. I asked him the other day if he ever played Trivial Pursuit. His reply: "Twice a month…when I pick up my paycheck."

He's still happily ensconced at the beach with an albino rabbit and a dark-eyed Parisian damsel. He's promised her he'd get his act together in '85. Of course, by then Barnum and Bailey may no longer be interested.

A few weeks ago, he was rear-ended coming onto the freeway but escaped unscathed. And yesterday he had minor surgery. Delicacy prevents my pinpointing the exact location, but if the doc had slipped we might have had a ballet dancer in our midst. It required some fast talking to get him in for the elective surgery. Like Woody Allen, he said he wasn't afraid to die—he just didn't want to be there when it happened.

"Skates" Doren, our athletic granddaughter, continues to win trophies as regularly as some people change underwear. Won a first place in city competition in July.

Like all 11-year-olds, Angela's hooked on video games and plays music with lyrics that are as understandable as Latin was for me. But she's a kick to have around.

Sherrie has had an exciting year doing expensive things with her Danish beau, Helge. He is a really class guy. And I'd like him even if he wasn't letting me use his fabulous penthouse condo on the Coronado Shores as a get-away to scribble on my book. (It has a view clear to Ensenada—the condo, not my book—and originally belonged to Willie Mays.)

Sherrie is into psychic phenomenon. Last spring, she was one of five contestants on a new TV pilot show taped here called *What's On Your Mind* with two top psychic readers, an astrologer, and Joanne Worley as guest star. Afterwards, the panel told her she was quite psychic herself.

So she's since taken up tarot card reading. She ran the cards on me the other night. I asked what she saw in my future. She said I would be poor and unhappy until I was 59. I asked what would happen after that. She said then I'd get used to it.

Daughter Debbie is dragging her feet on producing her first progeny. The hundred thou they say it will cost to see that the kid reaches 18 in good style is giving her sleepless afternoons at work. Still in insurance claims, I think she's about had it with new bosses, lawyers, and accident victims. Says the more she sees of her fellow man, the more she loves her dog.

Deb told us the other day the only money she and Billy ever save in these times is by drinking during Happy Hour.

Billy took over the mortgage loan firm he was a partner in after the final space cadet left. Brought in some high rollers as partners and plans to have the electricity back on by the first. His lawyer warned him last summer if he didn't bail out, he'd wind up with his picture on post office walls. Instead, there's a photo of him now in Mortgage Banking News.

I did something rather memorable to highlight my 1984. I didn't fall down while running the Olympic torch for SeaWorld. The boss apparently wasn't too sure I'd make a kilometer, though. He volunteered to have me run in Scapoose, Oregon, where I wasn't well-known. But it was a great thrill. Scapoose is a community of well-to-do farmers. They lined the road applauding, cheering and waving Gucci banners.

Actually, it was a moving and patriotic experience. Crowds lined the roads for 30 miles into Portland. I signed autographs for over half an hour. Mothers thrust babies in my arms for pictures. Women crowded around to touch my torch. (Oh, the thrill of it!) And the media interviewed me. I thought for a while I was running for mayor and gave a short speech.

Speaking of my boss, Mr. Schultz turned 50 this year and seems to have mellowed. His wife says he's been reading the articles in *Playboy* and cutting out pictures in *Time*.

We're going for the elusive three million in visitors for '84. Schultz admitted our publicity had something to do with it. My staff won the Public Relations Club top award for the penguin stuff we submitted. We won Best of Show award from the American Marketing Association chapter for our marketing and PR programs promoting the little strutters.

Schultz says getting publicity on these creatures seems to be so easy, I should wear a ski mask when I pick up my paycheck.

As a reward for 12 years of flacking for Shamu, he sent me to Cleveland in July. I did so well there, I was sent to Chicago during a blizzard in November. I'm afraid to do any better.

I still play a little tennis (won a sweater that doesn't fit in a hotel-motel association tourney) though I have an arthritic pain here and there. I'm still trying to convince myself it's the weather.

Took the usual amount of guff on my birthday. My secretary gave me a Sun City Workout book and a card that said Help Eliminate Wrinkles—Iron a Prune. She thinks she's so young and smart. But I caught her trying to use Wite-Out on the word processor.

Well, I wanted to tell you how my name appeared in *Newsweek*, about our dinner with Pulitzer prize-winning journalist and author David Halberstam, and our new TV documentary series with Leslie Nielsen. But it now seems like shameless boasting, which we try to avoid in these annual rantings. And my watch says it's a quarter past December. So I must send Lovae to the post office with this.

We both wish you the best and hope you have the jolliest ole season. In the New Year remember these words once written (by someone wiser than me): "What you cannot avoid—welcome."

Jingle Bells!

1985

Christmas music was playing as I stepped off a plane in Fiji last week. A gargantuan native warrior in a skirt and sandals swept around the terminal building and grunted "Bula!"—causing me to drop my duty-free package and pinch my ring finger in the revolving door. "Merry Christmas to you," I called back, only to find out an hour later from a bartender clad chiefly in shark's teeth that bula is simply "Howdy!" in Fijian.

Anyway, the next day I checked the Quantas pilot's breath and heart and completed my 12,000-mile trip from Australia home to launch the 20th annual holiday word purge for those of you too kind to ask me not to. But unless your packages are under the tree and the eggnog properly laced, you don't have time to hear about my year.

The still curious may ask what I was doing on Thanksgiving in the land of the hairy-nosed wombat, having turkey prepared by Aborigines. (Their dressing is just a tad too spicy!) Quite simply, I was a guest of the state of California, in Sydney for an international conference on lotteries.

For those of you who heard I left my 13-year post as SeaWorld's PR Director last spring and figured I was still on welfare, a tweak of the nose. For those just now numbed by the news, I should explain that I was appointed public affairs director of the state's big crap-shoot in June.

Suffice it to say, I will always have a whale-of-a-spot in my heart for Shamu, but launching a Lottery is the most fun you can have with your clothes on.

Don't ask how I landed the job. A cosmic plot was involved. (Sherrie, did you have a hand in this?) Larry Thomas, the guv's press secretary, once was engaged to my brother's major league pretty daughter, Linda. Larry, always a superior judge of character, said the Duke was looking for a flack with a few years' tread left, who believed in psychic reward, so he immediately thought of me!

I told my domestic goddess, Lovae, I would go to Sacramento just to have lunch with Larry, but I wasn't moving from San Diego, ever! I'm not sure what happened, but he obviously put something in my drink. Next thing I knew, the Lottery director fell for my line about making him a national icon—and Governor Deukmejian appointed me. He sent along an official wall certificate for which they're still trying to collect $5.

As all but a few tribes along the Amazon must have heard by now, our sales have gone off the graph. Over $21 million opening day, October 3. Over $80 million the first week. (In 1983, we boast in comparison, the veteran Ohio Lottery sold only $58 million instant scratch tickets all year.) One might say we created a $10 million a *day* business in six dizzying months.

By the time you've hauled your Christmas tree out for the trash collector, we'll have sold one billion tickets. A record that may well never be topped. I expect the Duke will knight my boss.

It didn't come easy, though. Twelve-hour days have been the norm—and I had to rent a second home in Sacramento. But it's been so danged exciting and rewarding my complexion's cleared up. Can you believe that in August and September, my press guy,

John Shade, and I handled 50 to 90 media calls a *day* and didn't become alcoholic in the process?

I run around the state giving speeches like I know what I'm talking about. If I don't get an offer to do a TV interview a day, I call Pacific Bell to see if my phone's been disconnected.

The governor, who was vocally opposed to the Lottery initiative, made a surprise appearance at our first capitol press conference to announce the start-up date. You might say he's taken a firm stand on both sides of the issue. (His favorite color is plaid.) Anyway, I did a portion of the dog-n-pony show that day before some 40 news types and 11 TV cameras. Set my anti-stress program back two months.

Now one of my fun tasks is to stand around a drafty Hollywood TV studio every Monday while a millionaire or two is made during a spin of a big game-show-type wheel. Winners to date have included such sterling personalities as a motorcycle-riding grandmother, two illegal aliens, a black garbage collector, a Vietnamese refugee on welfare, an Irish elf and a convicted thief. The press thrusts a mike in my face afterwards and asks: "Why?"

My personal favorite big winner was a young, good-looking bachelor from Santa Barbara. A news guy asked him what he planned to do with all that money. The kid thought a minute and said: "Well, I'll probably spend about 70 percent on fast cars and a couple blondes. About 20 percent will go for good Irish whiskey. The other 10 percent I'll probably just blow!"

The variety of new millionaires makes wonderful copy for the morning paper, though. The *LA Times*, which hates the Lottery, is forced to run us front page often, since we're hot stuff and there is so little war or disaster news these days. Consequently, we're getting more ink statewide than anything but AIDS.

Planning the statewide kickoff, as I recall, was right up there at the top of the max stress chart. With the help of my dynamic LA staff, under Randi Thompson, and San Diego's Dave Nuffer and his agency, we managed to spend a cool million on opening ceremonies, much of it on a star-studded show in the Hollywood Bowl with spectacular fireworks and laser show (including a fly-over by the space vehicle from the Olympics).

Steve Allen served as master of cermonies, introducing performers such as Vicki Carr, Don Knotts, Ann Jillian, John Schneider (*Dukes of Hazard*), Robert Guilliuame (*Benson*), Fabian, Frankie Avalon, Irene Cara, Anthony Newley, and a few others who straggled in after the USC marching band. I was out of intensive care in time to attend with my one-drink wife, who danced in the aisles after three splits of champagne. I may be heading south, though, when the boss sees the last of the bills.

I still get off on Hollywood. Even though working there is like being surrounded by a bowl of granola, as someone said. What's not fruit and nuts is flakes.

Before I joined the Lottery, I spent a few months in Las Vegas after being retained by George Millay, one of SeaWorld's founders, to help plan and publicize the opening of his latest water park, "Wet 'n Wild." We had a real gala after talking Dorothy Lamour, Debbie Reynolds, Rich Little, Esther Williams, and "Gomer Pyle" into making a splash with us! I had to postpone opening ceremonies an hour Saturday morning, because Robert Goulet's voice wouldn't work for the national anthem before 10:00 A.M.!

Debbie Reynolds liked Lovae a lot, hugging and posing with her. And Esther Williams called me four times at home to make sure I had a limo to pick up her and the family. A lovely lady.

Dorothy Lamour, now around 80, told me of her dates with Howard Hughes. "Such a sweet man," she said dreamily. "Sent me a single yellow rose after each date!" (I thought he could've afforded a whole bouquet!)

I flew the family to Vegas for the ceremonies. It was granddaughter Angela's first plane ride. The stewardess came by to ask how she was enjoying it. "Fine!" Angie enthused, gazing down at the vast desert below. "But I was wondering—when do we go over the Bermuda Triangle?"

For several months, I lived part-time in the Sahara Hotel, right on the Strip. So Sacramento, a pretty city with millions of trees, looked good to me (even though only a few degrees cooler!) But you sit in air conditioning, waiting for winter. And the fun goes on...

There's this AP reporter who could have lost Dale Carnegie as a friend. The other day, he called, grousing about the Lottery, then asked my opinion on why something so evil and with such lousy odds has become so popular with Californians. I fell back on a quote from Nick the Greek: "Man's greatest pleasure is gambling and winning. His second greatest pleasure is gambling and losing."

The lighter moments keep you going. Guy phoned the other day and wanted to know if I'd heard about the Lottery in Poland. I admitted I hadn't. "Well," he said, " I understand they give the grand prize winner a dollar a year for a million years!"

Our home in San Diego hasn't sold for taxes yet, so for the 25th year, an obscene number of gifts will wind up under our twinkling tree Christmas eve. Lovae's scrubbed and waxed the garage floor, painted the driveway and decorated everything, including the knobs on the toilets. Our tree is slightly over-dressed. No branches—just ornaments.

But I love the nuttiness of the season. Everyone smiles a lot. Like they weren't on a sleigh ride to bankruptcy. And I can't wait to see grandson Nolan ripping and slashing at all the packages, just as all my 18-month-olds have for the past 35 Christmas morns.

Gawd, but I'm daft about that kid. Fly home every weekend I can to work on his punting and receiving. (I don't know why we haven't heard from UCLA yet.) His jabber would make you believe there are alien beings among us. I can't understand a word. But we communicate. Like when he pulls my ear while I'm napping, it means it's time to feed the bunny again. Which we do about every 15 minutes. You ever seen an 80-pound rabbit?

Speaking of kids, my own heirs are outstanding. If you were wondering.

Gary hasn't finished junior college yet. He's only been there two terms—Carter's and Reagan's. He displays a vivid imagination and often thinks the CIA will respond to his letter suggesting changes in the application process. He gave up on his plan to raise mushrooms in China and has been working Wednesdays for a foreign importer of awnings.

Sherrie stays nimble trying to keep up with Angela as she approaches her teens. My athletic granddaughter (more skating trophies this year) made cheerleader at school—and regular chiropractic visits.

Last Christmas I said to Angela: "One day before we know it, you'll be all grown up."

She said: "You, too, Gramps!"

Pretty gnarly kid.

Sherrie gave Angie a miniature dachshund last Christmas instead of a sister. Critter's so small when he barks he sounds like a bagpipe in heat.

Sher broke with her well-to-do friend and maintains a happy, if slightly jaded, outlook on male relationships. Has a T-shirt reading "When God Created Man She was Only Kidding."

Craig and Dana presented us with Ashley Breanne, a 7-pound doll who will surely break a lot of surfers' hearts in the year 2001. Nolan won't let me spend much time with her yet. But I'm sure I'll be taking both to the zoo soon. Craig's construction company is still solvent, and he may unlock the secret to making a million on his own. I'm counting heavily on it.

Lovae, my rock, is still saying she hopes to live long enough to become a burden to her children.

Deborah Lovae Ray, daughter number 2, tired of shifting her mind into a state resembling brain death for three hours each day during her favorite "soaps" and returned to the work force. Their Black Lab ate the cable, so she wasn't getting good reception anyway. She assists hubby Bill in their now-thriving mortgage loan business.

When Billy isn't on the tennis courts in his free time, he's heavily engaged in fixing up their acreage to resemble something out of Bali Hai. He's moved so many rocks, the neighbors call him Fred Flintstone.

His son from a previous marriage, Matthew, 12, pitched and hit his way to All-Stars by early summer and got to pig out on fudge ripple ice cream. Admitted he's acquired a feminine admirer. "It's serious," he said. "She told me her last name."

My brother Mark (known to the family as "Bud"), a flower importer in Miami, has been rushing about South America, using guile and cunning to drive down carnation prices. He'll be joining us for the holidays, so I must go put away the good stuff.

We do miss seeing you. Geez, it would be great if we could do it all over again, wouldn't it? Just a little smarter.

Keep scratching…lottery tickets, that is!

I offer these words of wisdom for the New Year: "Never lend money to a friend. It will damage his memory."

Noel Again!

It's amazing how fun flies when you're doing time, isn't it?

Boggles my mind to think that the California Lottery is already into its second year of operation. The boss asked me to come up with something to commemorate our first anniversary in October. But I couldn't figure out how to frame an ulcer.

Don't take that wrong. M. Mark Michalko, Esq. is a great guy in my book. He has accomplished more in less time than any other Lottery director in history. Yet he remains a humble man. A very democratic man. He doesn't want anyone calling him "sir." He says kneeling is enough.

Surprisingly, the Lottery is still hot news in California. The director thinks I'm some kind of wizard. The truth is, our story is a good giggle for the slow news day, sandwiched in between the latest axe murder and hostage-taking.

Now if the legislators would keep their bony fingers out of our pie, life could be a bowl of cherries. But if God hadn't wanted people to laugh, He wouldn't have given us politics, they say. Mark claims bureaucracy is the turning of energy into solid waste.

He popped his youthful head into my office one early evening and asked if I'd like to attend the International Lottery Conference in Turkey with him in September.

A short while later, after reports the ragheads had shot up the Istanbul Synagogue and someone trashed the Bank of America branch, he said, "You go."

I packed and let the air out of his back tire before I left. PanAm helpfully showed the movie *Midnight Express* on the way over. I tried to breathe normal going through Turkish customs. My inspector looked like someone who did terrible things to small animals. But my 70 vitamin capsules and bag of powdered vitamin C was finally cleared.

On the bus ride through the dark, winding streets of Istanbul, everyone sat as if their chairs were wired for low-voltage jolts. My seatmate, a skinny woman made up like a Forest Lawn corpse, trembled with anxiety.

Istanbul proved to be a safe, historic city of six million dazed citizens trying to get across the street for a pack of cigarettes. I was nearly gassed in elevators, buses, restaurants, and telephone booths. Apparently they pluck the eyes out of anyone not caught smoking. My dentist asked the other day if I'd seen any camels. I said only in someone's mouth.

Between UN-type sessions with English, Spanish and French interpreters, we supped in scenic restaurants and toured blue mosques and marble palaces built by the horney Ottoman sultans. I complained bitterly but was never allowed, for some mysterious reason, near the harem rooms. Apparently, things are still going on there. I OD'd on feta cheese and Greek olives while checking out belly dancers on both sides of the Bosporus.

It was a hoot mingling with Lottery directors and marketing aces from 41 nations, sharing a universal problem: how to talk your citizenry into parting with a buck, a franc, a peseta, or a ruble for a good cause—your employment.

I was seated at a state dinner the final evening with the head of the Russian Lottery. They've had a sports Lottery for nearly eight years and launched Lotto a year ago. We exchanged pins and toasted with vodka glasses, and I informed him we had America's largest network of retailers—20,000 stores. He laughed and told his interpreter to tell me *they* had 64,000 in Russia.

A Japanese delegate sat on my other side. I learned that he was responsible for selecting Kamikaze pilots during World War II. I couldn't help asking how these young men were picked. He said: "I tell you. I read their palm. If they have a long lifeline, I send them home."

Did he think I just fell off the turnip truck, or what?

I've completely recovered from the three strains of virus I brought home and nurtured through our gala Lotto kickoff in mid-October. I helped launch the game in ceremonies at the San Diego festivities, along with Steve Garvey and Tony Gwynn, who forgot their lines, but showed up for their check.

Okay, get a big mug of black coffee and a pack of No-Doz as we continue the name-dropping session.

The following Saturday night in LA we announced the winning Lotto numbers to climax a half-hour live television show. It was a black tie affair. Lovae looked gorgeous in hers. Flip Wilson was MC and there were appearances by Milton Berle, Susan Anton (legs all the way to the floor), and Steven Bishop.

Last Friday, I was involved in a press conference at the Hollywood Roosevelt Hotel with Angie Dickinson, Mickey Mouse and that blonde who played E.T.'s mother. We have some wild plans for tying into the 1987 Hollywood Centennial Celebration. Disney people outlined a spectacular salute for halftime at the Super Bowl.

Staying at the restored Hollywood Roosevelt was a trip down memory lane. My child bride and I checked in there 27 years ago when I was looking for work and discovery as America's favorite unpublished novelist. The only discovery was how short of cash we were by Monday and the monolithic appetites California gave our kids.

Now those kids have their own kids, and Lovae and I have been married so long we're on our fourth bottle of Tabasco sauce. (We promised to grow old together, but the other day she told me *I* was going to have to slow down.)

I became a familiar face on the rubber chicken circuit the past 18 months in the course of beating the Lottery drum. I love the feel of a microphone in my slippery hand, my pulse hammering when they turn the TV cameras on. There's no excitement like it other than dangling on a fraying rope over a cobra pit.

I share with California audiences such nuggets of information as: If all the tickets we have sold to date were laid end to end, they would stretch not one, but four times around the world. (You don't have any idea how long it took us to lay out all those little puppies!)

I'm a tad bushed when I get home on occasional weekends; then wrestling those well-fed Gerbers grand babies who stay with us leaves me a semi-invalid by Sunday. Still, there was no call for my wife to write Dr. Ruth and ask if it's legal in this state to sleep with a corpse.

I took the hint and whisked her away for a few days to distant lands. Following a Lottery confab in Seattle, we drove up to Vancouver to exchange our IRA for EXPO. We found color, excitement, big crowds, and five days of really wet rain.

Then we made one of our infrequent returns to the shores of the Potomac in the spring. Had a downright orgiastic reunion with Clint McCarty, John Ford, and other good friends from our *Navy Times* publishing days, where I was a reporter in the '50s. Also, dined with my first boss and mentor in the PR field at NAREB. It was nearly 80 degrees and the cherry blossoms were out and everyone was boasting about the four seasons in the East.

I said, "San Diego has four seasons, too: early summer, summer, late summer, and next summer."

Son Gary and his girlfriend have a sharp-looking used Mustang now that they drive back and forth to the repair shop. Their other car was so old the DMV issued it upper and lower plates. He and his lady share a surfboard and some spectacular sunsets at their rental in Ocean Beach. Gary says retirement is so much fun, he decided to do it while he was still young enough to enjoy it.

I don't know why I didn't think of that.

Daughter Sherrie spent the summer luxuriating in suburbia. Her place of business vanished because the owner didn't much like the mob and gambling element beginning to congregate in the steak house. They threw a big party on their last night. Highlight was a drawing in which the grand prize was a Thompson machine gun.

She's back working lunches at a bustling new restaurant and has been voted amateur magician of the year. She's able to be at work, the super market, the skating rink, school, and the kitchen all at the same time.

She and boyfriend Dick have fixed up a great view home in the Mt. Helix area, which their sausage hound, Critter, enjoys as her castle. Speaking of castles, my 13-year-old granddaughter, Angela, was named Queen of her junior high at the dance Wednesday night. Sherrie is walking around like Queen Mother.

Angela grabbed off a few more first place honors in skating and has started a second trophy case. Guess that jinxed her. She finished seventh in state finals.

Number one son, Craig, recently moved up to join a top-quality San Diego home-builder. He claims his last supervisor was the only living brain donor.

We're embarrassingly attached to his kids. I have custody all weekend when I'm home. I give up Chargers and Padres games to babysit (okay, so that's not the world's greatest sacrifice anymore!).

At 2½ and 1½, they experienced their first Halloween. Mom Dana took them trick-or-treating in our neighborhood. Nolan was wearing a horrible mask when a lady answered the door and exclaimed, "Oh, what an ugly face!" Quiet, unobtrusive Dana called out from the curb, "He looks like his father!"

Actually, Craig looks pretty good for someone approaching middle age. He is tanned and lean and has gotten in good enough shape to eke out an occasional tennis victory over his Dad.

He says my grandchildren are so spoiled, they think child abuse is being denied ice cream for breakfast.

Daughter Deborah and husband Bill drink Corona beer and take yuppie-type vacations to Maui and Puerto Vallarta as business continues to boom for them. Lovae watches the store when they do. One of the salesmen watches Lovae.

Deb went under the knife several months ago in her gallant and continuing quest to make little Debbies. Billy just can't eat any more oysters. He chanted and burned incense every night she was in the hospital.

Meanwhile they race half-way across the county watching Billy's son Matthew play Pony League baseball, where he's an All-Star, and now in JV basketball.

Billy put a bumper sticker on their sporty red Mazda: "The Meek are Contesting the Will."

My brother moved his import operation to New Orleans and flew here for turkey sandwiches. He has grown a magnificent gray beard, which hasn't fooled the IRS for one minute.

My mother approaches 85 with a gleam in her eye, claiming to have three boyfriends at the nursing home. She can't figure out where I am and occasionally calls the police to report a kidnaping.

My crack sidekick Bob Taylor, just phoned to say we had an $18 million Lotto winner from the San Diego area. I must run for a plane (they keep one on the runway for me). I hope to get back in time to see Iowa romp in the Holiday Bowl.

Merry Christmas to you from our whole flock.

Let's get together in 1987 for a power lunch.

In the New Year remember this thought from W. C. Fields: "Start every day off with a smile and get it over with."

Yuletide Greetings!

1987

As sure as the sun passes from horizon to horizon in the sky above, here comes Rudolph—and my letter again.

And, lord love a duck, another round of holiday parties. I pray the medicos have better success with liver transplants soon. Or that they at least find a cure for hangovers before the 31st. I can't take another one like last New Year's. I finally groped my way over to Dan Grady's for the traditional watching of the Rose Bowl game, icing my skull—which felt like the skin had been stretched over a football—eyes pulsating like radar blips, stomach churning.

Robin Schmidt said I should drink a warm glass of gin with a horse hair in it. I lost it…right there in the flower bed.

My daughter, Deborah, claims sleeping in is the best hangover remedy. "After all, that's why God made January 1," she says. Her husband, Bill, claims sex is the best thing—if you can find someone without a headache.

I'm a little sensitive about writing you this year. My wife gave me Ann Landers to read yesterday morning with my Captain Crunch. Miss Landers condemned all Christmas newsletters as egotistical exaggerations of events recalled by dim people desperately needing to top your year. Or something equally encouraging.

But that's really not what we're dealing with here. I don't have the creative powers to make *my* year sound better than yours. I realize I have a month to go in which I could still win the Lottery, but then we all know about those odds (they are tattooed on my wrist).

Actually, the year was not devoid of events worth recounting. It's just that I woke up this morning depressed and aching. So I checked my horoscope in hopes of finding an uplifting message. It said: "You will catch your mate answering a personal ad."

Okay, I know you're not that interested in my travels and awards. You'd rather see Sophia Loren or Paul Newman naked. But here are a few highlights:

Lottery director Mark Michalko and I did our soft-shoe routine before stunned audiences of hundreds in Austin, Texas, and San Francisco to launch this "transition" year of 1987. I later traveled to Orlando, Florida, and Honolulu, to spread the gaming gospel— not to mention a knock-out luncheon in Bakersfield, California, where I kept 90 dazed Rotarians awake with unprovable statistics.

I posed for photos with Magic Johnson in the locker room following a Lakers' game, and later was taken by my boss to the opening NBA playoff match at the Forum on the promise that I wouldn't talk about the time I played with Bill Fitch (hometown Cedar Rapids, Iowa, star, and veteran NBA coach).

In March, I was one of the San Diego Press Club Headliner-of-the-Year recipients (along with our lady Mayor, Chargers coach Don Coryell, Rolf Benirschke, Charlie Jones of NBC, PSA airline's Paul Barkley, two Mexican nuns, and a scientist). My acceptance speech did tend to run on. But less than a half dozen people wandered off to the rest rooms.

Told them one of my great pleasures in this job is seeing people go from "struggling to make their car payments" to being a millionaire in a matter of moments. I said Don Coryell told me he sees that happen every spring with the Chargers.

(That got quite a laugh from the audience. Can you handle one more?)

I grabbed a first place in the annual Lottery public relations awards for the best promotional event in North America in 1986 (the Lotto kickoff with Flip Wilson, et al, orchestrated by Randi Thompson, my LA public relations whiz). The handsome plaque was presented at a dinner for 600 during the national convention Lovae and I attended in Montreal. What an anniversary present to give your wife! She's hoping for a matching tennis trophy for our 40th anniversary in June. Or a diamond and emerald tiara.

Lovae flew from San Diego to meet me in Montreal. I had called ahead from Sacramento to a hotel and asked for a nice room. They quoted me a bargain rate of $195 a night. "I'm bringing my own girl," I argued. "Is it still $195?"

The big news was that in July, while feeling hostile from caffeine, the director and I resigned from the State Lottery to form an international Lottery management group, with temporary offices in Texas.

I left my dedicated, talented, overworked staff following a major, heartwarming, tearful farewell party in Sacramento, which the governor and several hundred other notables were unable to attend. But for the 12 of us, it was a heavy scene. All agreed that since I had no real direction in life and could no longer make it to the office before 10:00 A.M., consulting would be an ideal position for me.

While Mark used his boyish charms to try lining up several fantastic contracts and throw the Mafia off the trail, I went home to work on my long-ignored novel. So I have been lapping up the warm December days and the extended writing vacation. I took my three-year-old grandson, Nolan, to the beach last week. A plane went over towing a banner. "That plane," he announced, "still has the price tag on."

He cracked another one after I finally produced on a promise to take him on his first train ride, a 20-mile jaunt up to Del Mar for lunch. He asked what the men were doing looking under the train as we boarded. One had a mallet, so I told him they were probably giving the wheels a whack before we could start. Later, as we got up to full speed, the car dang near shook us silly. Nolan said solemnly, as his Coke sloshed around: "They better stop this twain and give those wheels another whack!"

Which reminds me, other than trips to the supermarket and the doctor, granddaughter Ashley, two, has never been exposed to the outside world, except visits to Little League and football and baseball on TV. Son Craig and wife Dana took her and Nolan to the Big Top in August. Dana asked Ashley what she thought of her first circus as she was putting her to bed. "That was a really good ball game, Mom," Ashley replied.

Craig is doing well for a guy who used to think Chicken Little was right. He's helping build executive-style homes in the North County and making a Yuppie type salary. He just moved the family into a small existing home in Ocean Beach, still near enough for us to get frequent hugs from the little people. Craig was saying the other day that behind every successful man stands a surprised mother-in-law.

I reminded him of what my daddy told me: "Work hard and save your money, and when you are old you will be able to buy the things only the young can enjoy."

Gary, 24, still harbors hopes of breaking into the movies. So far, it's only been through the side door at the Loma Theater. He thinks going back to school might be a neat thing to do between surfing sessions. Like Reagan, he tends to treat reality as an illusion that can be overcome.

His girl still drives the vintage Thunderbird, whose clutch has given out three times since 1986. She claims it will do 0 to 60 in 30 minutes.

Eldest daughter Sherrie was despondent for a while during the summer. She read a survey that said a single woman over 35 had about as much hope of finding a husband as she had of winning the Publishers Clearing House Sweepstakes.

But that Pepsodent smile is back on her Cover Girl face. She's been discovered by a young man who reads without moving his lips and has a well-developed sense of humor. They seem to have fun doing little things, like trying 100 dishes with chunk tuna.

I asked my granddaughter, Angela, how she can go out there as a solo in the spotlight in sequined tights and $300 skates before a hushed crowd and zip and leap around in an intricate routine without missing a beat, or falling on her peaches and cream complexion. I liked her answer: "Winners see what they want to happen. Losers see what they're afraid will happen."

Deborah Lovae Ray, daughter number two, is still undergoing experiments by men in white coats and thick glasses in an attempt to get preggers, a decision that has puzzled many friends. "Debbie," they said in unison, "you are blessed with a good job, a loving family, and a dog that has stopped jumping up and mopping your face—why would you want something that wets and spits up on you?"

But she has a need for something to cuddle now that her husband has a new computer and comes home from the office late. Billy is still trying to figure out the cursor, which he claims was invented in a Transylvania lab by someone named Igor.

B.C. (before computers) Bill fixed up their Lakeside place in a rustic, enviable, and frankly embarrassing manner. Every time he puts in a new sprinkler system or rocky retaining wall, Lovae pinches me and wants to know why I can't do something useful like that. I'm afraid I'm the kind of guy who always hits the nail right on the thumb.

In the summer, Lovae put on her babushka and went to Russia after losing her annual battle with the snails. Actually, she, her perky mother, sister, and brother took a Royal Cruise Line tour of England, Holland, Russia, Finland, etc. Lovae enjoyed Leningrad and Stockholm, especially, and brought back 900 photos and a cough that lasted until Thanksgiving.

In spite of a broken toe, she let her hair down at Dan Grady's birthday party. He poured her glasses of French champagne and fine wine. Because he refuses to act his age, it was a smashing party. Dave Nuffer called the morning after to say his hair hurt and he couldn't feel the enamel on his teeth.

She thoughtfully bought me a gift from a bookstore in London: *Sex Over Sixty* in the large print edition. I don't mind these age barbs. I prefer to think of myself as sort of an apprentice senior citizen. (My favorite part of the newspaper now is "Twenty-Five Years Ago Today.")

One thing about aging, you doubly enjoy seeing and hearing from old friends. We had great visits with ex-Navy pal John Moen and Ori in Hawaii; dinner before the Holiday Bowl here with the Schraders (Gus was my first sports boss at the Cedar Rapids Gazette); brunch in Orlando with Clint McCarty (my roomie in Spain 30 years ago) who's an editor at the *Orlando Sentinel*; and an entertaining dinner with the Zoo's famous ambassador Joan Embery and hubby.

A friend from my *Navy Times* days sent the best flash of the year. Said he had it on authority that Tammy Bakker has entered the Betty Ford Clinic for cosmetic dependency.

Meanwhile, the only excitement I've had in a month of Sundays was as a result of the geographic plates shaking under California. With the big rattle occurring at 5:00 A.M., I hardly remember yelling, running past Lovae and over the cat into the backyard.

Well, carry on outrageously with Santa and the plastic. And maybe tip one to our memory at year's end.

Watch for us in the headlines. Maybe we'll make a splash in '88—even if Shamu doesn't!

I leave you with a thought from my Lottery colleague, Bob Taylor, warmed by this fortune from a pack of Bazooka bubble gum: "Even a broken clock is right twice a day."

Arrivederci, amigos.

Give the Gift of

Humorous Letters From the Edge

to Your Friends and Loved Ones

CHECK YOUR LEADING BOOKSTORE OR ORDER HERE

❑ **YES**, I want _____ copies of *Humorous Letters From the Edge* at $12.95 each, plus $3.95 shipping per book (California residents please add 97¢ sales tax per book). Canadian orders must be accompanied by a postal money order in U.S. funds. Allow 15 days for delivery.

❑ **YES**, I am interested in having Bill Seaton speak to my service club, company, association, school, or organization. Please send information.

My check or money order for $_____ is enclosed.

Name _____

Organization _____

Address _____

City/State/Zip _____

Phone_____ E-mail _____

Please make your check payable and return to:

Green Flash Publishing
3466 Larga Circle
San Diego, CA 92110

For bulk quantity discounts, please call 619-222-9982